WHO OWNS THE ICE HOUSE?

Eight Life Lessons From An Unlikely Entrepreneur

by Clifton L. Taulbert and Gary Schoeniger

WHO OWNS THE ICE HOUSE?

Eight Life Lessons From An Unlikely Entrepreneur

ELI Press, LLC
7340 Lauren J Drive Cleveland, Ohio 44060

For information about bulk purchases of this book or the Ice House Entrepreneurship Program, please contact info@elientrepreneur.com

Library of Congress Cataloging-in-Publication Data has been applied for.

ISBN 978-0-9713059-1-5
1 2 3 4 5 6 7 8 9 0

For Jason,
who inspired this journey.

For Uncle Cleve,
whose life told us it was possible.

"Our deepest fear is not that we are inadequate. Our deepest fear is that we are powerful beyond measure. It is our light, not our darkness that most frightens us. We ask ourselves, 'Who am I to be brilliant, gorgeous, talented and fabulous?'

Actually, who are you not to be? You are a child of the universe; your playing small doesn't serve the world. There's nothing enlightened about shrinking so other people won't feel insecure around you. We are born to make manifest the glory of all that's within us. It's not just in some of us, it's in everyone.

And as we let our light shine, we unconsciously give other people permission to do the same. As we are liberated from our own fear, our presence automatically liberates others"

— MARIANNE WILLIAMSON

WHO OWNS THE ICE HOUSE?

Eight Life Lessons From An Unlikely Entrepreneur

TABLE OF CONTENTS

Foreward by Thom Ruhe . . . . *xi*

Preface . . . .*xvii*

Introduction by Clifton Taulbert . . . . *xxv*

Chapter 1: CHOICE *33*

Chapter 2: OPPORTUNITY *59*

Chapter 3: ACTION *75*

Chapter 4: KNOWLEDGE *89*

Chapter 5: WEALTH *105*

Chapter 6: BRAND *123*

Chapter 7: COMMUNITY *139*

Chapter 8: PERSISTENCE *155*

Afterward *169*

Acknowledgements *177*

FOREWARD

As an entrepreneur, mentor and life-long advocate for entrepreneurship, I have long searched for meaningful education programs for entrepreneurs. Specifically, I sought something that could convey the essence of an entrepreneurial mindset and the limitless opportunities it could provide. More importantly, I wanted to know—from successful entrepreneurs—the beliefs behind the behavior that led them to achieve the success they now enjoyed.

In my capacity as director of entrepreneurship at the Kauffman Foundation, I have the good fortune to travel the world; being exposed to every manner of entrepreneur support groups and the programs they offer. From Brazil to Bangladesh, I have seen first hand, that entrepreneurship has become quite popular and the "secret" of our American entrepreneurial spirit is not so secret anymore as countries around the world are awakening to the benefits of an entrepreneurial driven economy.

Yet, while entrepreneurship programs have begun to emerge on college campuses and in small business development centers across the country and around the world, the

Clifton Taulbert and Gary Schoeniger

traditional academic, institutional approach has met with limited success. Many rely on a textbook-classroom format that tends to focus on the mechanical aspects of entrepreneurship such as business planning, cash flow projections and market research while overlooking the underlying beliefs and assumptions that enable entrepreneurs to succeed. Others are limited by the lack of relevant curricula or experienced instructors who understand and are able to articulate the true essence of entrepreneurship and what it really takes to start and grow a successful business. Moreover, there is no formulaic approach to entrepreneurship and attempts to do so have repeatedly proven to fail. While many programs provide basic technical information, they often lack the real-world insight and practical skills that only experienced entrepreneurs can provide.

Therein was my motivation to find and fund an education program that was derived from first-hand experience, extracted from the tacit knowledge of those who have overcome hardship and adversity through entrepreneurship. I was searching for a program that could not only inform but one that could inspire the next generation of individuals pursuing their dream of building a better life for themselves and others. And so it was that I discovered the Entrepreneurial Learning Initiative. Little did I know, they happened to be in my own backyard.

"Don't you live in Mentor, Ohio?" began a conversation with the Kauffman Foundation's VP of Communications, Wendy Guillies.

"I sure do, why do you ask?" I replied.

Wendy went on to explain that one of our news-feed clipping services had picked up a short article about an entrepreneurship training program being offered by a company called the Entrepreneurial Learning Initiative—ELI for short—and they were based in, of all places, Mentor, Ohio, my hometown.

Turns out, ELI had been founded and was operating less than 3 miles from my home, a slight embarrassment for me to admit as I had never heard of them.

ELI founder and co-author of this book, Gary Schoeniger, enjoys retelling the story of my first call to him as rather suspicious. "Who are you and what are you doing in my backyard?" he likes to credit me as saying—with a smile. Whereas I know that he has an embellished recollection of that first exchange, I have to concede that I was more than a bit curious about their activities in the community I had been entrepreneurially serving for many years.

Gary was polite, if not forthcoming with details of their activity, so naturally I asked for a meeting to learn more about what they were all about. It was at our first meeting that I was relieved to find out that I didn't know about them because they were, for all practical purposes, a start-up themselves, having recently released their first public course; Mindset: Tapping Your Entrepreneurial IQ.

The course is an online video curriculum featuring entrepreneurs from a diverse background of ethnicity, gender, age, and means. From a woman who transformed her hobby into a thriving business after losing her job, to serial inventors and some of the most successful entrepreneurs of our time, Mindset was like no other entrepreneurship education program I had ever evaluated. What made it unique was the unfiltered sharing of experiences from actual entrepreneurs that, in their own words, describe what they went through and what they endured or overcame to get to their current station in life. They share with the student all the things I wish someone had told me before I took that first journey down the entrepreneurial rabbit hole.

Clifton Taulbert and Gary Schoeniger

For the first time, I could see someone taking THIS course and being better prepared for all the things they don't teach you in the nuts-and-bolts courses. Beyond the mere sharing of the experiences, Gary and his partner Mike Sutyak had extracted, in consumable bites, the tacit knowledge that drove these successful entrepreneurs—*the beliefs and assumptions behind their behavior.*

As my own entrepreneurial endeavors were colored by many good and difficult experiences, I was confident that they had decoded the entrepreneurial DNA in a way that anyone, from diverse backgrounds, could learn and, more importantly, launch more confidently knowing that challenges lay ahead but nothing was insurmountable.

It was in my own taking of the Mindset Course that I was first introduced to co-author, Clifton Taulbert. In the course, Clifton refers to the inspiration he received from his Uncle Cleve; "He was different in his community because he actually took money to the bank."

Why did that make him different? What was so special about this man that made him a standout in his community? And perhaps most importantly, how did this man's life influence young Clifton Taulbert to become an award-winning author and a successful entrepreneur?

The answers to these questions became the foundation of this powerful book and companion course. Taulbert and Schoeniger do a masterful job at identifying the eight life lessons from an unlikely entrepreneur, Clifton's Uncle Cleve, while providing high-impact context these lessons have to empower this generation to overcome adversity through entrepreneurship, while leading the economic recovery the world is waiting for.

We feel privileged to have had a small role in bringing this powerful program to our nation's greatest natural resource, our entrepreneurs. It is my hope that others will be inspired by this story and empowered to take control of their destiny and to create a brighter future for themselves and others.

THOM RUHE
Director of Entrepreneurship
Ewing Marion Kauffman Foundation

Clifton Taulbert and Gary Schoeniger

PREFACE

E ntrepreneurship is a mindset that can empower ordinary people to accomplish
the extraordinary. Entrepreneurial success does not require
a revolutionary new idea, a Harvard-approved business plan,
or millions of dollars from a venture capital firm. The same
life lessons that fueled blue-collar working class Sam Walton
of Wal*Mart, college dropout Steve Jobs of Apple, public hous-
ing resident Howard Schultz of Starbucks, and countless other
powerful and successful entrepreneurs are within reach of
every single one of you reading this book. As entrepreneur and
author Chris Gardner said, "You gotta dream. . . . You want
something? Go get it." Gardner wrote the book, *The Pursuit of
Happyness,* and was portrayed by Will Smith in the movie of
the same name, which told the story of how Gardner overcame
homelessness and adversity through entrepreneurship.

Opportunities do not always come with identifying signs
screaming: "I AM AN OPPORTUNITY. COME GET ME!"
Sometimes they are more subtle.

The meeting of the two entrepreneurs who wrote this
book was one of those more subtle moments, one that almost
did not happen. Gary Schoeniger and Clifton Taulbert met

Clifton Taulbert and Gary Schoeniger

on a very busy day in the spring of 2008. Gary Schoeniger, an entrepreneur, was in the process of conducting video interviews with entrepreneurs throughout the United States as part of a project sponsored by the Cisco Entrepreneur Institute, in which Gary was supposed to gather as many in-depth stories of as many successful entrepreneurs as possible. But Gary wasn't looking for any old entrepreneur, he was focusing on those who had started out behind the eight ball, pushed themselves beyond what they thought was possible—and certainly beyond what anyone expected of them—to the kind of success that all entrepreneurs strive for. Gary was looking for the Outliers.

Gary himself had not come from promising beginnings. He was a miserable student who barely graduated high school, taking odd jobs here and there to survive. Good with his hands, he often landed at construction sites where he found he had a facility for carpentry. But he never made a steady or reliable living. One day out of sheer desperation, he strapped his carpenter's ladder onto his beat-up truck and started driving around the neighborhood, offering his services to those who needed their gutters cleaned. Within months, the gutter cleaning service evolved into a handyman business that he ultimately transformed into a successful construction and development company. Gary Schoeniger knew what it was to start from nothing, to push himself, to strive to be the best in a niche where he could succeed, and he ultimately became a successful entrepreneur.

Having made his mark, Gary became interested in helping others. He adopted a foster child, Jason, caring for and mentoring him and ultimately launching Jason into the world where he went from being a kid with a bleak future to becoming an entrepreneur himself. Jason got Gary to thinking: If I could do it and if Jason could do it, what about other kids? Gary first began to teach entrepreneurship to high school kids, in the process culling together yet more stories of entrepreneurial success—this time from kids who had not yet even reached voting age! Then he began lecturing to adults at entrepreneurs conferences, taking what he had learned and sharing it with educators and others. That soon evolved into Cisco Systems approaching Gary and asking him to prepare an online course in which he related many of the success stories he had gathered over the years. That eventually led Gary to Tulsa, Oklahoma.

One of the people interviewed was Clifton Taulbert.

Born to a teenage mother in the 1940s, Clifton lived with various caring relatives while growing up. His childhood in the Mississippi Delta coincided with the age of Jim Crow – the system of legal segregation that created few opportunities for success, much less gainful employment. When he was 13 years old, Clifton was hired by his uncle, Cleve Mormon, to help out at his uncle's Ice House, the only one for miles around. Everyone needed ice, and everyone came to Uncle Cleve's Ice House. So Clifton met everyone. Black, white, Chinese, Jewish—everyone was treated the same by Uncle Cleve; they were all customers, all welcome. Clifton watched his uncle very carefully. The lessons he learned from his Uncle Cleve ultimately propelled Clifton into entrepreneurship himself, where over time, he became part of an investment group that started a successful bank in Tulsa. He was nominated for the Pulitzer Prize, and was even profiled by *Time* magazine as an outstanding emerging entrepreneur. From humble seedlings spring promising possibilities.

Clifton Taulbert, a black guy from Mississippi, and Gary Schoeniger, a white guy from Cleveland shared very similar stories. But neither of them knew it. Yet.

While interviewing in Tulsa, Gary kept hearing the name Clifton Taulbert. But he was already so booked, he had no time to hunt down another interviewee. Nonetheless, someone managed to introduce Clifton to Gary. Soon, the camera was set up, the lights were adjusted, and two strangers found themselves sitting across from one another in a crowded conference room. Little did they know this meeting was the beginning of a mutual journey that would extend far beyond that room.

The journey started out with Gary's question, "Clifton, who influenced you to become an entrepreneur?" Clifton answered by telling Gary the story of his Uncle Cleve. This man had been a major influence in changing the trajectory of Clifton's life. Memories flooded in, and as Clifton, a natural-born storyteller, continued relating the real-life tales about his uncle, Gary listened with an intensity that could be seen all over his face. His eyes looked as if he had actually traveled back to that small community and had personally shaken hands with the man who had owned the Ice House. Such was the power of Clifton's storytelling.

The resulting interview was brief, but Gary was hooked by Clifton's stories about Uncle Cleve. If there ever was one of those more subtle opportunities that make themselves known over time, this meeting qualified.

With the interview over, the video equipment packed up, Gary and Clifton shook hands and said goodbye. As far as Clifton was concerned, that handshake signaled the appropriate ending to a completed project. Clifton had shared his story; Gary had recorded it. Both men returned to their respective responsibilities—Clifton in Tulsa and Gary in Cleveland—running their own small businesses. That afternoon, the interview did end, but the relationship had just begun.

Within weeks, Gary was on the phone with Clifton, keeping him abreast of his interviews around the country. Over the next couple of months, their phones continued to keep them in touch, and their conversations about Uncle Cleve and his rather unique role as a business owner gathered more depth. The interview, now extended into cell phone conversations often late at night slowly made both men aware of just how significant the working life of this ordinary man had been. Through Gary's persistence and insight, an opportunity emerged that same year for Clifton to share Uncle Cleve's story at an international entrepreneurs conference in Austin, Texas. As Clifton recalls:

> I'll never forget that afternoon speech in Austin. The place was packed. As I got ready to speak, I kept thinking about Uncle Cleve and wondering how his life would come across to this audience. He was no tycoon. No buildings were named after him. No one had written an article about him in the Wall Street Journal. He left no great wealth for distribution among his heirs. He was a simple man who chose to live differently.
>
> I was a bit apprehensive. In my head Uncle Cleve occupied an honored place. He was respected. I wanted no less for him at this conference. His black and white picture—a period picture, no less, and my only picture of him—kept rolling through my head. This would be the picture the audience would see. I would be hurt if this photograph elicited laughter instead of respect.
>
> I remembered his life and the many things about his life that I had once just taken for granted or assumed were personal gifts just for me. It was sobering to think that now those conversations and words of wisdom from a different century were being recalled for others. Fortunately, my fear was unfounded. As I finished my talk, Uncle Cleve was welcomed with a standing ovation. Gary was right. Uncle Cleve's message was universal.

At the conference in Austin, Uncle Cleve's story and his tenacity and commitment to personal success was recognized and embraced by the crowd as timeless. As attendees shook the two men's hands, Clifton and Gary were in awe at the reception of Cleve's story and its relevance to 21st century entrepreneurs and students exploring the possibilities of entrepreneurship. This ordinary man from a different time in history had awakened the spark of possibility within many of the conference participants.

Gary and Clifton left Austin feeling good that they had at least been able to bring Uncle Cleve to such an event. They shook hands once again to go their separate ways. But it soon became abundantly clear that their "goodbye" would be short lived. They continued to call each other, always talking more and digging deeper into the extraordinary life of this very ordinary man. No conversation ended without some reference to this unlikely entrepreneur. It was during one of those calls that they conceived the possibility of developing an online multimedia course for aspiring entrepreneurs and for anyone who wanted to unleash their potential and provide value for themselves and for others.

Who Owns the Ice House?—the question initially posed by Gary during that first interview—became the name of the project.

Who Owns the Ice House? today includes this book and a companion online course. In this book, the authors have tried to capture the impact Uncle Cleve's life had on a young boy, then thirteen, and on the working and mentoring relationship that exposed that boy to new possibilities for a future beyond the fields of the Mississippi Delta. This relationship became the perfect backdrop for probing into the universality of the entre-preneurial mindset that allowed Uncle Cleve to defy the odds and to bring young Clifton along on his journey. The mentoring relationship and the long-range impact of Uncle Cleve's lessons are brought to life through the personal stories Clifton tells in this book. Clifton then proceeds to elucidate the impact the story held on his own entrepreneurial development.

This unusual framework then turns to Gary, who draws from his decades of personal entrepreneurial experience, to carefully and thoughtfully elucidate from each of those Ice House stories the key entrepreneurial points and their contemporary relevance, illustrating them with further accounts of entrepreneurship.

Who Owns the Ice House? is a collaborative effort in every sense of the word. Entrepreneurship does not always have to be a lonely, solitary journey. *Who Owns the Ice House?* is a tribute to the many ordinary men and women, boys and girls all over the world, who, like Uncle Cleve, are refusing to give up on their dreams and slip away into obscurity. It is dedicated to those who are determined to make their lives count. Years ago Uncle Cleve, a man who always drove the speed limit, showed us all what is possible today.

Clifton Taulbert and Gary Schoeniger

INTRODUCTION BY CLIFTON TAULBERT

If you want to maximize your innate potential, whoever and wherever you are, *Who Owns the Ice House? Eight Life Lessons From An Unlikely Entrepreneur* is for you. This book is about the entrepreneurial mindset—a way of thinking and being that is life changing. Welcome! Your future is important to us. Your future is important to the society in which you live. More importantly, your future must be important to each of you.

Now, more than any other time in history, the future we share together as humans will need our all-hands-on-deck commitment. And no one embraces the future like the entrepreneur. They seem to have an aversion to sitting on the sidelines. They welcome the challenge. What is their secret? What drives their day-to-day actions? Is their code for success accessible to everyone?

The answer to all these questions is a resounding, *Yes!* In *Who Owns the Ice House?* we deconstruct the "entrepreneurial code." We take you inside the success stories of various entrepreneurs and down the roads they traveled. You, too, will learn the "code." This book and its online course can become your personal roadmap for unleashing your potential to achieve your best.

Clifton Taulbert and Gary Schoeniger

Being an entrepreneur is a dream embraced by many people all over the world. We recognize the entrepreneurial journey as that of an individual who, in spite of challenging circumstances, rises to incredible success. We stand alongside them on their journey and cheer them on. We admire their tenacity. We celebrate their determination. We rejoice in their success.

But oftentimes, we see them from a distance as the archetypal jetsetter: powerful, influential, and far-removed from our own lives and ambitions. For some, the word *entrepreneur* conjures an image of the tech-savvy Silicon Valley wonder-kid with an Ivy League diploma, or better yet, as someone born with unique abilities one either has or does not. As much as the ideal of becoming an entrepreneur is admired, for many, the embodiment seems out of reach. Uncle Cleve had neither special privileges nor abilities to draw on, yet he was able to leave a legacy of entrepreneurship that left its impact far beyond his own life. He was an ordinary person—just like us, just like you. With nothing to recommend him other than his will to succeed, Uncle Cleve shaped his life into the perfect vehicle for understanding the entrepreneurial mindset. Did Uncle Cleve possess something that no one else could access? This is the question that drove Gary's and my collaborative efforts in our mutual endeavors.

The more we dove into the life of this unlikely entrepreneur through emails and one-on-one conversations, the more we became convinced that the entrepreneurial mindset that had guided Uncle Cleve's life and the lives of business entrepreneurs the world over, also had potential for guiding and impacting a wide range of behaviors pertaining to both youth and adults. Yes, the entrepreneurial mindset had been instrumental in Uncle Cleve's business success, but we also saw greater potential within this entrepreneurial mindset that was waiting to be explored and applied. Uncle Cleve possessed no secret potion. But we both immediately noticed the powerful,

WHO OWNS THE ICE HOUSE? *Eight Life Lessons From An Unlikely Entrepreneur*

transformative influence of his journey on *both* our lives. Gary witnessed its impact on the young people who had crossed his path. I experienced it in my own life. Together, we decided that the entrepreneurial mindset was too great to be relegated to just one aspect of our lives—starting and growing businesses. We knew that the entrepreneur possessed a mindset that moved him or her beyond challenging circumstances, setting him or her apart. Like a bolt of lightning from the sky, we understood that this mindset had multiple applications and the potential to provide the requisite subtle shift in thinking that allows entrepreneurship to flourish. From personal experience, we understood that to think differently is to also act differently. That shift had happened in our lives. It had changed our perspective. It continues to drive our actions. This is what we want for you: your potential unleashed for the good of your communities, and for yourselves.

Our next steps became clear: We needed to find a partner who could see what we were seeing, that is, who could understand and support the power of the entrepreneurial mindset to change lives. That partner became the Ewing Marion Kauffman Foundation of Kansas City, Missouri—an organization respected all over the world for their commitment to ensuring the presence of entrepreneurship in America and beyond. Once we gained the support of the Kauffman Foundation, our real work began. We were determined to bring the Ice House of the 1950s to life and introduce to the world the wisdom that was contained in Uncle Cleve's experiences. Armed with the combination of Gary's twenty years of work in the entrepreneurial corridor and my life experience with my Uncle Cleve, we set out to develop this project: to write the book, distilling Uncle Cleve's ideas into eight lessons, and to create the online course that would capture the stories and wisdom of 21st century entrepreneurs.

Clifton Taulbert and Gary Schoeniger

Each chapter in *Who Owns the Ice House?* has four sections. In sections one and three, we will take you on a personal journey into the Ice House—introducing you to my world through my stories and observations as well as through those that convey Uncle Cleve's impact upon my adult life. In sections two and four in each chapter, Gary will draw from his experience to provide the key mindset lessons lived out by Uncle Cleve as well as the modern-day application of those lessons and the opportunities they can provide. This collaborative project will explore the timelessness and universality of Uncle Cleve's entrepreneurial mindset lessons for today's enterprising youth and adults as well as for the restless reader simply seeking direction. *The Ice House project is designed to set you on a course to discover the timeless truths of these lessons that will galvanize your will to maximize your potential.* This is what Uncle Cleve demonstrated through his work at the Ice House and during his life in the Mississippi Delta.

We want you to know this humble man, to experience his words of wisdom and lasting examples of how to unleash your own potential for success when life's circumstances are telling you otherwise. These mindset lessons from more than a half-century ago have become particularly relevant in today's economy as millions have lost their employment, and all of us struggle in an increasingly uncertain, unsettled world. The K–12 educational system is being challenged as never before. Budget cuts and lower test scores leave our youth far behind their peers in other developed countries. Young people are dropping out in unprecedented numbers, and the achievement gap between the various ethnic groups is widening. And yet, among the chaos and confusion that has marked this new century, technology has brought about an era of unprecedented opportunity, and a spirit of innovation and experimentation has gripped us. From this, good outcomes can happen.

This book introduces you to Uncle Cleve's secret: the mindset that is just waiting to become part of your daily life—whether you are running an Ice House in the Mississippi Delta, or starting a small business in Detroit; whether you make your living working at a large organization in Los Angeles or in a classroom in Tulsa; whether you are a single parent or someone who is looking to make a fresh start. The entrepreneurial mindset is transformational when embraced and experienced on a daily basis. We have witnessed its ability to move ideas from speculative notions to realities—in spite of challenging circumstances. We also know that this mindset offers a new way in which to view the world, one that reveals new opportunities, ignites ambition, and unlocks your innate, untapped human potential.

It is our hope that *Who Owns the Ice House?* will reshape your image of who an entrepreneur is and what it takes to succeed. In *Who Owns the Ice House?* you will be introduced to the entrepreneurial mindset lessons that guided Uncle Cleve's life, the very same lessons that continue to guide successful lives today. Not only will his story change your idea of what an entrepreneur looks like, but it will also expand your understanding of the extensive impact of the entrepreneurial mindset. We hope this book and its accompanying online course will stir your imagination and enable you to recognize opportunities that are within your reach wherever you are. We hope to unleash something within you that will allow you to rise above your circumstances, whatever they are, and create the success that resides within you.

The world has changed dramatically since the 1950s. The reality Uncle Cleve knew will never exist again. However, the lessons from his life are timeless. This project—the book and the online course—comes at a time when people are trying to succeed in the face of overwhelming odds. And yet, although

Clifton Taulbert and Gary Schoeniger

we may be fearful when we start out, we are also hopeful. This book is written to capitalize on that spark of hope. When hope was in short supply in the Mississippi Delta, Uncle Cleve, an unlikely entrepreneur, found the way to grow a little hope into his own business and have control over his own destiny. Bringing *Who Owns the Ice House?* is his legacy, his gift, to you. He is surely telling all of us that if he can, you can too.

For some people, the most difficult thing to do is to change or to think differently about their lives, to think differently about their future. They have become accustomed to sameness. Gary and I know better. Because of what we've experienced in our own lives, we know that you don't have to do the same unproductive thing one more day. To change, to turn around, to expect something different for your life—this is your right. Claim your rights! It will not be easy. It's hard work, day in and day out. Uncle Cleve tells us that hard work is the road that leads to independence. He never called himself an entrepreneur. The term did not exist in his time, but the concept certainly did. You'll find out that he had a smile that never quite broke out across his face, but this little knowing kind of grin hinting that he knew something that others perhaps did not. In this book, we take you behind that knowing grin. We take you to work with him and his nephew. You'll sweat with them, and you'll go to the bank with them, and you'll finish high school with his nephew. You'll see the entrepreneurial mindset at work.

The great advances in human history—as well as in our own lives—rarely come about as the result of doing more of what we are already doing. The great advances come about as the result of a shift in our awareness—that little grin that indicates we have seen something different for our lives. I was 13 years old when I was first exposed to the grin that would lead me to Uncle Cleve's powerful transformational principles—principles I have continued to practice throughout my life.

These eight mindset lessons know no boundaries. They are not held captive by race, gender, geography, or time. They are not reserved for the powerful and the privileged. They do not require an Ivy League education, unique talent, or technical ability. If you desire them, they are yours for the taking. These are the lessons we offer:

Lesson 1: **CHOICE**
Lesson 2: **OPPORTUNITY**
Lesson 3: **ACTION**
Lesson 4: **KNOWLEDGE**
Lesson 5: **WEALTH**
Lesson 6: **BRAND**
Lesson 7: **COMMUNITY**
Lesson 8: **PERSISTENCE**

We have embraced these eight entrepreneurial mindset lessons as our own, and we invite you to do likewise. Become part of the future—a growing community of those who still dare to dream and are willing to put in the time needed, exert the effort necessary, and pursue the knowledge required.

Our book, *Who Owns the Ice House?* concludes with an Afterward—a heartfelt conversation from both of us— that takes you beyond the Ice House. We want you to know that in America, You Can Own the Ice House! —however you define it. Our goal is to provide you with tools to discover and maximize the potential within you. The entrepreneurial mindset is the gift that any of us can access. Once accessed, it keeps on giving—from one generation to the next.

CLIFTON TAULBERT
November, 2010
Tulsa, Oklahoma

WHO OWNS THE ICE HOUSE? *Eight Life Lessons From An Unlikely Entrepreneur*

CHAPTER 1

CHOICE

"I learned this, at least, by my experiment: that if one advances confidently in the direction of his dreams, and endeavors to live the life which he has imagined, he will meet with a success unexpected in common hours."
—HENRY DAVID THOREAU

"The mark you make today will show up tomorrow."
—UNCLE CLEVE

CLIFTON'S WORLD IN THE MISSISSIPPI DELTA

"**C**liff! Go on and git up, boy! Git on outta that bed. The sun's already up an workin'. It's time to wash up and git your food. You know, you cain't be late for work. My brother-in-law, Cleve, won't stand for that. I wuz talking to Cleve on Sunday while visiting him and my sister, Mae. That's when he told me all 'bout his decision to hire you." Those were the words I heard early one morning in 1958, that day I partnered my young life with Uncle Cleve and his Ice House more than 50 years ago.

33

It still amazes me that a conversation and a job that happened so long ago could end up being so impactful on my life . . . even today. The picture is as clear in my memory as the day I heard my great aunt's voice yelling out to me from the small kitchen and into my small bedroom. My new job and her commitment to my life came together to forever change my perspective of who I could become. Before I take you to the Ice House and to Uncle Cleve, I want you to understand what the world around me at the time was like so you can see just how fateful my job at the Ice House would become.

It was the summer of 1958 when Ma Ponk's words pulled me off my small cot to get ready for work. It all happened so long ago, but it seems like yesterday when my mind travels back to Glen Allan, Mississippi, where I was born. It was a small cotton community, way off the main highway, with a population of less than 500 people, located on Lake Washington. Cotton fields stretched as far as one could see, both literally and figuratively.

Limitations, social, physical and emotional, were all around us.

Just thinking about my hometown brings back memories of the insufferable heat and humidity that were constant during the summer months and necessary for growing cotton. Even as a young boy, I recognized the extent to which cotton shaped our lives. I can remember when there was nothing else to do but sit on the top steps of my great-grandfather's front porch and look out as far as I could see. I wanted to see something different, but all I could see was Greenfield, a plantation community just south of us, the same place I had seen all my life, with the same

WHO OWNS THE ICE HOUSE? *Eight Life Lessons From An Unlikely Entrepreneur*

rows and rows of cotton that looked as if they would never end. Even then, that sight made me think that I was seeing the end of my world. Limitations, social, physical and emotional, were all around us.

I grew up during the time when cotton was still king, and our lives were defined by strict racial segregation. It was a restricted world with so many boundaries in place, that is until my great aunt entered my life. She took it upon herself to raise me, to make sure that I accomplished something useful. Until I met her, I lived in different homes with various relatives, starting with my great-grandparents. I had been born to a teenage mother and my future was uncertain—or certainly limited. That was until Ma Ponk altered the course of my life forever.

For Ma Ponk, teaching me to work hard was part of her commitment to my future. Working hard had brought her a measure of independence. She wanted the same for me—and more. Sleeping late was never tolerated; thus, the memory of her admonishment to "git up" still rings in my ears. I was only thirteen, but within our southern culture, I was man enough to do a full day's work. Ma Ponk never had to call me twice. I was slow to move, but always up before she had to yell at me for the second time.

That morning in June 1958 seemed like a typical workday; however, it would turn out to be very, very different. I was going to work—but not to the cotton fields where I had been working for several years and where she, herself, would go that day. No, I would not be bending low in the hot sun from early morning to sunset, carefully weeding the young cotton plants—a process we called chopping. Uncle Cleve, Ma Ponk's brother-in-law who owned the Ice House, had offered me the opportunity to work for the summer—that is, *if* my first few days worked out to his satisfaction.

35

I remember the day Uncle Cleve's truck slowed down and stopped beside me. I was walking uptown, but he motioned for me to come over. "Clifton, I been watchin' you. You got a good head on your shoulders. Ponk's doing a good job in raisin' you. I been giving this some thought. How 'bout you coming to work for me? What you say, boy?"

I was dumbfounded that day, hardly mustering up the words I needed. "Yessir, yessir, Uncle Cleve! I'd really like that. I know I can do it."

With his ever-present pipe in his hand, he opened the door of the truck and invited me closer, somewhat laughing, but not quite. "Now hold on, boy! The work is hard. You gotta git up early. You gotta be on time! I know young 'uns like you. You like to sleep late. I ain't havin' none of that. I'm telling you now, if you late, more than two times, you cain't work for me."

I assured him that I could do it. He reached out and shook my hand just like I was a fully grown man. I remember smiling to myself and slowly walking away. I did look back once and I saw Uncle Cleve slowly driving his truck down the street and into his front yard, parking in the same place he always parked. I could hardly wait to get back home and tell Ma Ponk.

I was just another "field hand"' even though I was barely a teenager.

With my new job opportunity, I was ecstatic, and so was Ma Ponk. She was happy that her boy would no longer be a "field hand," as we were commonly called. She wanted something better for me, and so she was determined that I would be on time. Uncle Cleve had a reputation for being on time and expecting the same of others. He made no exceptions. All throughout Glen Allan this was common knowledge. I was eager to start, and Ma Ponk was committed to making sure that I made a good first impression. "Boy, git outta that bed!" Those were her words that June morning that started my day and introduced me to a way of working and thinking that would forever shape my life. I will never forget that morning, the day I no longer had to catch Mr. Walter's field truck as it headed out to the cotton fields with the field hands.

Mr. Walter's truck had been picking up people for field work and taking them to surrounding plantations for years. Getting on his truck had become a shared way of life. This was what we did, continuing a system that was an outgrowth of slavery—the human labor force needed to support the massive plantation systems in the south. When I came of age to chop cotton, it was no different for me. Mr. Walter's truck showed up without fail. Ma Ponk and I were among his faithful customers. We knew to get up early before the sun rose to be ready when Mr. Walter's truck turned the corner by the colored school. Without fail, during those hot summer months, we would be waiting for him by the front gate. He never had to wait for us. Fortunately, Ma Ponk was a "mother" in the local church and as such was treated with respect. Mr. Walter always saved a place for her in the cab of the truck, but not for me. I was just another "field hand'" even though I was barely a teenager.

I had to crawl onto the back of the truck and fend for myself as I looked for a place to squeeze in. It never failed; I always stepped on somebody's foot or elbowed someone in the chest while trying to find myself a place to fit. "Boy, cain't you see? Git yourself some specks." I'd get the talk, but never a smack. After a while, the feelings would cool down, and we'd be on our way to the next stop. Laughter, jokes, and conversations I should not have heard at my young age soon filled the back of the truck. We were on our way, packed together like sardines in a can, so close that our steaming breath inter-mingled in the cold morning air. After several more stops, we finally made it to the fields where we would be given sharp-ened hoes and assigned cotton rows to weed. We never had to worry or think about when to start work because a whistle would blow or we'd hear Mr. Walter's loud voice telling us it was starting time.

"Alright, all of y'all, wake up. Git on wid it. Git yore rows. Jim, git yore water buckets ready, and be careful, don't waste my ice."

> *Nothing was required of us except muscles and time—no thinking, no planning, no creativity—just the rhythms of tending to cotton that had been part of Delta life for generations.*

Knowing it was time to start, we would let our laughter die down, and the adults got really serious about the only work many of them had ever known. It was no different for me. I also knew it was time to become serious. With my row assigned, I would bend low, as I had been taught to do, and carefully look for weeds to cull out that were hiding among the young plants. This would be our backbreaking routine for the next ten hours. This was our way of life. Except for a precious few, all of the people in our small community made their living from doing field work. Nothing was required of us except muscles and time—no thinking, no planning, no creativity—just the rhythms of tending to cotton that had been part of Delta life for generations.

However, that hot day in June, I broke with tradition. I did not catch Mr. Walter's truck. I had a job. Working in the fields was never called a job. It was just what we had to do. Upon hearing of my great luck, the older people who knew me expressed their pride and their expectations. "That'll be good for the boy. Cleve'll teach him sumpin'. Sho' hope he can hold out, though." My being able to leave the fields boded well with them, but they knew Uncle Cleve's reputation for hard work. Some of my young friends teased me about my job because Uncle Cleve was known as a no-nonsense man—a man who barely ever smiled. I didn't care. I wanted that job. I was tired of field work. I never wanted to earn that admired reputation of chopping more rows than anyone else. I never wanted to learn how to sharpen my own hoe. Even though I was born into that world, I always wanted something better. I didn't know what better would look like; I just knew that I wanted something different. The problem was that "better" jobs were virtually nonexistent—that is until the job at the Ice House opened up for me. I couldn't wait to be out of the scorching sun. For me, Uncle Cleve's reputation as something of a taskmaster was no impediment. Hard work didn't scare me. Ma Ponk had raised me, after all. She even made up work for me to do when none really existed. No matter how hard or no-nonsense he may have been, working for Uncle Cleve in the Ice House had to be much better than the fields.

He lived in our neighborhood and was
subject to the same social restrictions
as the rest of us.

Clifton Taulbert and Gary Schoeniger

I don't know much about Uncle Cleve's early life, where he was born, or about the personal hardships that he may have encountered along the way. I just knew he came from Coldwater, Mississippi. I am sure, though, that he never went beyond grade school, if that. Even so, he could read, write, and count, and he possessed an incredible memory. All of this and more came to light as I spent time in his presence. Later, I would learn that nothing could get past him. Yet, apart from owning the Ice House, he was one of us. He lived in our neighborhood and was subject to the same social restrictions as the rest of us. He had no special gifts. He had no access to wealth. He was not related to special people, but he stood out from all of us. In our world where over 90 percent of our adult population worked in the cotton fields, he was among the few who dared to count his own dream as worthy of being pursued.

> *He was among the few who dared to count his own dream as worthy of being pursued.*

I always quietly admired Uncle Cleve. His courage and determination did not go unnoticed. Nearly everybody in our community called him Mister Cleve. I had taken notice of that. And he was respected. Just like us, he got up early every workday, before the sun rose, and went to bed late—but the difference was that he was doing it for himself. He was his own boss. He paced everything, even his driving. He always drove the speed limit or below it. I can still see him in his 1947 International pickup truck slowly backing out of his drive onto the gravel road that would take him to the Ice House. Some of the townsfolk laughed at his slow driving, but he never got into a wreck, and he always made it to his destination on time.

I thought he even walked differently than the rest of us. Uncle Cleve held his head slightly to the side as he ambled at his own pace, his ever-present pipe clenched between his teeth. He may have walked slowly, too, but he always looked as if he had somewhere important to go. Not only was he respected, he was also respectful. During the time when most of the adults in my community were being undervalued, Uncle Cleve's value of himself was shared among us. He always tipped his hat to the ladies and nodded at the men he knew, careful not to use language that was inappropriate. His confidence and the way he carried himself even impacted the white community's response to him. His actions defied stereotypes and so earned him a measure of respect, and whatever encounters there may have been were civil. While other men of his age were hanging out, getting involved in baseball, and making serious visits to one or two of the juke joints in Glen Allan, Uncle Cleve spent his time reading books, working on cars in his garage, or repairing one of his rental houses. Yes, this short, stocky, dark-skinned man who barely smiled and who was always working became a hero to me long before I went to work for him.

Sunday was our day off with many of my afternoons spent at Uncle Cleve's and Ma Mae's modest home. Uncle Cleve had this big chair in the front room that had everything he needed at his fingertips, his paper, his glasses, his can of Prince Albert Tobacco, and a cup of coffee, black, with no sugar. "Hey boy, whatcha doin' for yourself? Mae, you got somethin' for the boy to nibble on back there? Boy, you gittin' big. Still working everday when you ain't in school? Work is good fer you, course you know that. It keeps you outta trouble. You staying out of trouble, ain't you?"

"Yessir," I managed to utter. And before I could say anything else, he would be talking again.

"They's plenty of trouble for young boys to git into 'round here, but I been watching you. Real proud of the way you carry yourself. Ponk say you doin' good in yore studies. Keep it up. You gotta do right early and then keep it up. Sho wish I had your chances, boy, no telling what I could do." He looked so smart, all leaned back in the big chair and with the smell of his tobacco filling the room. I was captivated to say the least.

I was a young boy, but I admired his sense of independence, which seemed so different from many of the people I knew and loved. His conversation was always about being successful. He was one to always bring my schooling into the conversation. He made education an important topic. He always took time to ask me important questions about the world around me. Even before I went to work for him I wanted to be like him. Just watching him, I was unsure of how this could happen. However, once I started at the Ice House, this would all change. My excitement about working for a boss that looked like me was huge.

Glen Allan had not changed in a hundred years. Segregation was still the law of the land. Mr. Walter's field truck still picked up the field hands. But my world had changed. In the crowded cab of Uncle Cleve's pickup truck or on the days when the two of us talked while sitting on the bench of the Ice House porch, my thinking began to shift. While cutting and lifting blocks of ice and sweating profusely in the process, I learned to expect more of myself. Being in the presence of Uncle Cleve and observing the way he carried himself on a daily basis provided me a different set of lens through which to view my own life and potential.

Uncle Cleve refused to let his environment dictate his response to his life and his dreams—which was harder to do than not. Looking back, I know that he intentionally chose how he would respond to his circumstances. His life was his choice. There

42

is little doubt that his background and his environment influenced his life, but he did not allow it to determine the outcome. He chose differently. He knew he was black, but he also knew that his life mattered. It seems as if owning the Ice House provided him the necessary courage to venture even further in the world of business. By the standards of that day, he wasn't supposed to do any of this. Yet he continued to reach for the next step on the ladder. I saw him reach with my own eyes. It was amazing to me then, and even more so now that I realize the difficulty he faced because of the times in which he lived. All this must have given him a tremendous sense of personal pride, but he never wore it on his sleeve. He had that slight smile that seemed to indicate he knew something no one else knew, that he had a secret. But it was no secret that Uncle Cleve was all about his customers. He never forgot that the Ice House and his other businesses depended upon them. I learned from him to keep my priorities straight: The customer always came first. His actions were powerful lessons.

I was a young boy, but I admired his sense of independence, which seemed so different from many of the people I knew and loved. His conversation was always about being successful.

Cleve Mormon had stepped beyond what was expected of the people within our community. He showed me what was possible. Over time, I began to understand that I could do no less. My future became important to me. Although for four years I had to travel more than 100 miles round trip each day to high school, I graduated as valedictorian and with a perfect attendance record. Getting up to make the trip to school each

Clifton Taulbert and Gary Schoeniger

day and working hard to get good grades was not difficult for me. While at the Ice House, I had seen the value of working hard. I realized that my life mattered. I could add value to the life of others by making sure my life had value.

The day Uncle Cleve hired me was one of the milestones that changed my life. I broke with tradition. I was no longer squeezed in on the back of the field truck. I walked away from the established routine and took a chance that my work would please Uncle Cleve. For several years after, I would work at the Ice House during the summer, after school, and on Saturday mornings, working by his side and learning from him.

I arrived on time for my first day of work and every day thereafter. I was never late. Ma Ponk made sure of that. I started out clean and immersed in Mum deodorant. This freshness would not last long. The sweat would eventually wash it away, and be replaced by pale strains of salt. Uncle Cleve was determined that I would not let him down. He demanded much of me. "Cliff, come on, boy! Them field trucks will be here anytime now. Go on and cut up at least five 50- pound blocks of ice. That's what most of 'em'll git. It'll last 'em till noon."

"Yessir." Without any more talk, I was back in the Ice House, cutting and separating the blocks of Ice as I had been told. "Uncle Cleve, you want me to cut some 25 pounds?"

"No need to. I'm pretty sho they gonna want the 50-pounds block. You soon gonna be able to figger that out fer yourself. Now, you jus' 'member to hold up yore head, smile, and be respectful. You cain't hold no conversations with the people on the back of the truck. You got a job to do."

He had already shown me how to cut the ice, and he stuck with me until I could do it as well as he could. I think he forgot that I was not even 14 years old. But I knew how to treat people and how to be respectful, especially in a world defined by the laws and expectations of legal segregation.

I'll never forget his conversation on how to deal with our white customers. "Boy, we in the south. I know you know that, an' it kin be hard to deal with some of the stuff, but you kin do it. When the white customers come, you jes be polite. No matter what they say, you hold yourself. If it ain't good, then it aint 'bout you."

I just sat and listened and watched him over time. Looking back, I know it must have been difficult for him. He was amazing in his ability to keep his cool. By then I knew the routine of being an ice man, even the social aspects of how to comport myself. It wasn't easy work, but I was determined to succeed. Uncle Cleve had taken a chance on me. But more importantly, I had taken a chance on myself. I traded in my cotton sack and my sharpened hoe for an internship position with the owner of the Ice House, which in turn became the jumping-off point for the rest of my life.

Upon graduating from high school in 1963, with Uncle Cleve's blessing and that of Ma Ponk and the rest of my family, I headed north to St. Louis to continue what the Ice House experience had sparked in my life. I already had faith in myself and expectations for myself beyond the ordinary.

UNCLE CLEVE'S MESSAGE

The ability to choose the way we respond to our circumstances is perhaps the greatest power we have. It is a power that Clifton's uncle, Cleve Mormon, demonstrated throughout his life:

- *He had not a single advantage to claim over any of the others within his community and most were exposed to the same opportunities, yet many were simply blinded by their beliefs.*

- *He had no financial advantage—Uncle Cleve did not come from a wealthy family nor did he have access to venture capital investors or credit from a local bank. At that time, most banks would not even consider lending money to an African American.*

Uncle Cleve was an ordinary man whose only advantage was his mindset

---

- *He had no intellectual or academic advantage—Uncle Cleve was a simple man of average intelligence who displayed no particular genius. Although he could read and write and he understood basic math, he had no specialized knowledge, technical training, or other skills to set him apart. His formal education likely did not extend beyond the sixth grade.*
- *He had no political advantage—Uncle Cleve had no government contracts, inside knowledge, or special connections that enabled him to succeed.*

Uncle Cleve was an ordinary man whose only advantage was his mindset, a mindset that enabled him to choose a different life that allowed him to triumph over adversity as an entrepreneur.

It was his mindset that awakened his curiosity and opened his eyes to the world around him. It was his mindset that enabled him to recognize opportunities that others could not see. It was his mindset that ignited within him a desire and determination that empowered him to triumph over adversity and succeed as an entrepreneur. Ultimately, it was his mindset that set his spirit free.

ANKLE DEEP IN DISH WATER

Leaving the Mississippi Delta in June 1963 for St. Louis was the start of my life's adventure—one that would always have me looking back to the Ice House for encouragement.

We arrived at the train station early. It was going to be my first train ride. I was leaving the only home I had known for the unknown of the big city. With my high school diploma in hand and the knowledge learned at the Ice House under my belt, I felt I was prepared. I was proud that I had met Uncle Cleve's standards. What more was there to do? I could hardly wait to show the city what a country boy could do. However, that mid-morning day was bittersweet as I stood in the section of the "coloreds-only" waiting room, watching the Illinois Central pull in.

Ma Ponk was there to advise me. She had taken several train rides before. Like many of our relatives, her oldest son and several of her sister's children had moved to Michigan to work in the automobile industry. Ma Ponk was the relative who'd gone up there to check them out and make sure they were indeed doing well. She knew what to expect on my ride. She made sure I knew that once I crossed the Mason-Dixon Line, I would no longer have to deny my humanity. All the "whites only" signs would be gone. I could freely move around just as any other human being would.

"Now boy, you keep yore money in yore socks. People got long, narrow, reachin' hands on that train. I'ma gonna introduce you to the colored porter; he'll make sure you do what's right and don't git in no trouble. Now things are gonna change a bit when you cross the Mason-Dixon Line, but till then you just sit tight like we done taught you."

That was Ma Ponk: the same voice that had started me on my incredible journey with Uncle Cleve. Needless to say she had been proud of my work at the Ice House and had made

47

sure that all my cousins knew that I was selling ice. But now I was leaving Glen Allan and all that it had provided me. I was scared, but excited, too.

When it was finally time for me to board the train, I hugged Ma Ponk and my other family members as if I would never see them again. I wanted to remember their warm breath against my face and to pull some of their strength into myself. I was introduced to the porter and shown my seat. Soon the conductor was yelling, "All aboard! All aboard! Last call!" I was seated by the window where I could see my family as the train pulled away from Greenville.

The monotonous rhythm of the train soon lulled me to sleep. Unfortunately, when we finally crossed the Mason-Dixon Line, I slept through it. I was unable to see or feel the magic Ma Ponk had promised. I was still "colored" when I awakened, but I did notice that colored people had moved up from the back and into other coaches further up in the train. I remember how nice the porters were. That was the most important thing to me. Ma Ponk had told me that they could be trusted. Once in St. Louis, I was met at the Union Train Station by the birth father I had never known. Our meeting was strange, but filled with expectation on my part. I thought he would embrace me just like I imagined the big city would.

My first days up north were spent getting acquainted with new relatives who were slow in welcoming me and mighty vague when it came to solidifying my living accommodations. They were, however, quick to discuss how my rent would be paid. Right off, I knew that I was no longer the child at Ma Ponk's house or the boy at the Ice House where my work ethic had made room for me. It was over discussions about rent that I realized my survival would depend upon my getting a job sooner than later. My birth father had another family now, and I soon learned that the circumstances of my birth would not make me a welcome addition. I was in the city, but away from the family that really loved me. My father did find a room for me with distant relatives I didn't know. I was in the city, north of the Mason-Dixon Line, but it was not at all like I had fantasized. My city family was interested in little more than the rent I could provide. I was virtually on my own.

Applying for jobs and handing out resumes were all new to me. I didn't need those to board Mr. Walter's field truck or to work at the Ice House or at the grocery store. In Glen Allan, they took Ma Ponk's word and Uncle Cleve's recommendation. In St. Louis, I had neither. By now, much of my excitement began to drain out of me. I began to have doubts. Back home, working at the Ice House had been my badge of honor, but here in St. Louis, it was turning out to mean very little—or at least that was my thinking.

In spite of my fears and moments of doubt, I was still determined to be successful. I knew I could be, but I didn't know what success would look like in the city. Within days, for the first time in my life, I started scouring the newspapers for jobs, not even sure of what I was doing or how to determine my qualifications. I went on interviews at the recommendations of others, but they all turned out to be dead ends, probably not helped by my nervousness. I felt alone and without an anchor, no Uncle Cleve or Ma Ponk to give me that smile reflecting their confidence in me.

Finally, after weeks and weeks of job searching, a new friend from the church I attended helped me obtain a job at a large downtown department store that had a big public cafeteria. I was hired to wash pots and pans. I was hurt and disappointed I hadn't found something better. It only paid 35 dollars a week. While in Glen Allan, I had moved beyond such traditional and common labor. I didn't have to chop or pick cotton. I was Uncle Cleve's assistant. I ran the Ice House when he was off delivering ice. I waited on customers. I counted money. I tallied up at the end of the day. I was responsible for and closed up the moneybox. People knew my name. I knew their names. I had a real job. Washing pots and pans was not the dream I had when I left home, but I had no choice. I knew I had to work. I had to pay rent.

The first day I saw my new workspace—a small, isolated room with no windows and just an entry door—I felt as if cold water had been dashed over my hopes. I just stood there and stared. I had never seen such a mess. The room was piled high with dirty pots and pans crusted over with food and more food. It would be my job to clean them all. I said nothing to the friend who had helped me get the job, but inside, I felt as if I were back in Glen Allan chopping cotton. Only this time, the field was this isolated room where disgusting dish water was sometimes almost ankle deep and where my work uniform smelled of the discarded, spoiling food.

While stuck in that windowless room, I felt as if my job was a place from which there was no return. Unlike the excitement at the Ice House, which was always filled with people and provided an active social atmosphere, at the cafeteria my co-workers never really talked to me—especially those who worked on the food line. The pots and pans guy wasn't in their class. I was pretty much alone except for the times when the door to my work room would swing open to admit a large cart filled to capacity with yet more dirty pots and pans. "Here," was all the person said before he quickly turned and walked away. My job was so disgusting that it held people at a distance and kept conversations from materializing. Week after week, I waded through dirty water while washing grease-filled pans and scrubbing dirty pots.

It was during those trying weeks, when I was barely seventeen, that I really began to draw upon the lessons Uncle Cleve had taught me. In my isolation and loneliness, rather than focus on my uncertain surroundings, I let my mind wander back to those days with him in the Ice House. I would go through our conversations in my head over and over. His words became comforting and energizing. I recalled his talks about setting your own mind to get something done for yourself. Though I was in greasy water up to my elbows in the pots and pans room, I pictured myself riding in the cab of his truck or sitting on the Ice House porch, hearing his voice ring out. He talked and I listened. While scraping leftover meatloaf from a large industrial pan, I was delivering ice along with him and listening to the wisdom he dispensed.

It was during those trying weeks, when I was barely seventeen, that I really began to draw upon the lessons Uncle Cleve had taught me.

"Cliff, hard work is hard work, but now take y'all, yore generation, you kin do better then me and mines. Gotta keep gittin' book knowledge. Fill your head up. We didn't have that opportunity. I try to tell 'em all 'roun' here, but few of the youngsters listen. I's jus' an old man sellin' ice. But I done seen plenty in my time and thangs ain't gonna stay the same. Gotta be ready though. Be your best, boy. Jus' like I hired you here wid me, somebody else gonna see your good standing and 'fore you knows it, you done moved on up."

It was all coming back to me, working to dissolve my disappointment and restoring my confidence in myself.

I'm not sure how that first job in St. Louis would have affected me had I gone to it straight from the cotton field. Being at the Ice House had changed my attitude, increasing my sense

51

of self worth. It had given me a new look at what was possible in spite of what had always been done. At the time, I didn't know how to articulate all that was welling up inside of me and what I innately understood. I just know that more than my body had boarded that train in June of 1963. Something deep inside of me had come aboard too and was now coming to my rescue. I knew now I didn't have to settle for that dishwashing job. Uncle Cleve was telling me that. I knew that I could do more. I had done more before. I had to find a way to get a better job. Maybe I was looking for a new Uncle Cleve to help me usher in my future.

Washing pots and pans became my parking spot and during all that time on my own, I figured out my next move. Somehow my expectations for myself—the picture of my future that had emerged while at the Ice House—were coming to bear. And over time, these images and expectations began to guide my thoughts and actions. Every spare moment I could squeeze out of my day, I looked for a new job—and nearly every day, I was turned down. It was hard to put on a happy face when I experienced times of hurt deep inside of me. I couldn't give up. I couldn't go back home. I had to make it work. When I remembered my work with Uncle Cleve and his example, I felt empowered not to settle for less. Something better had to be out there. So I continued my search. I had to find the road to my future.

And, just when I thought all hope was lost, I got a big break. Yes, such moments do occur. A young Jewish job recruiter pulled me aside after an interview and asked that I come back to his office after hours. He had a job possibility. I returned to the office at the time he specified. I didn't know the recruiter was Jewish until I returned. I just assumed he was a white guy. But as we began to talk, when he told me he was Jewish, I remembered the Jewish family back home. They were different, and so was he. He seemed to know I was capable of more. The job being offered was at Jefferson Bank and Trust. I knew all about this bank. It was in the news every night. It was at the heart of the city's civil rights movement. In fact, the movement, then led by young William Clay, had captured the attention of the national media—especially when their demonstrations brought a halt to the building of the now famous St. Louis Arch, which was designed to symbolize the gateway to the freedom of the west. Because of new desegregation laws, Jefferson Bank and Trust was under a court-ordered mandate to modify their hiring practices. Now they were actively seeking employees of color. This guy thought I could fill the bill.

So with his help, I completed a resume of sorts and filled out an application, leaving it for him to usher it through the appropriate channels. This was all so new to me. All I could do was to wait and see and hope while I continued my job washing pots and pans. I wasn't sure if the job would come through, so I continued to look around for different work while I washed and waited. Finally, I got a call back from the recruiter. The bank wanted to interview me! I was really nervous, but I was ready. After all, I had been valedictorian of my class and had virtually run the Ice House.

During the interview, the interviewer quizzed me a lot about Mississippi, school, and my life in general. With the detail they made me go into you would have thought that I was being hired to be the president, not just a mere employee. With the interview over, we shook hands and I left. I returned to my washing and scrubbing, all the while allowing myself a tiny spark of hope that I would be able to leave this smelly, confining room.

At last, the call came that moved me out of the kitchen. I was hired by Jefferson Bank and Trust. My hiring resolved many of the civil rights issues the bank had been facing, and

I was out of the dishwashing room! I was no longer going to the field. I was on my way to the bank. I was unsure of what I would find, but I was setting out on a new path in a new city. And I was more than ready.

THE TIMELESS APPLICATION

"It ain't what you don't know that gets you into trouble.
It's what you know for sure that just ain't so."
—MARK TWAIN

The ability to choose the way we respond to our individual circumstances is perhaps the single most powerful ability we have as human beings. It is also a fundamental concept that lies at the core of an entrepreneurial mindset. Rather than reacting to our circumstances, we all have the ability to choose the way we respond. It is a subtle yet powerful distinction, yet it is one that many overlook.

We all make assumptions about the world around us. We make assumptions based on our experiences and observations. We often buy into the collective mindset of those around us. We make assumptions based on what we may have been told or encouraged to believe yet have never really tested for ourselves.

We also make suppositions about our own abilities: about where we fit in, what we are capable of, and what we deserve. Yet, here too, we often do so without ever really challenging these ideas. And by doing so we may be accepting limitations—limitations that are actually self-imposed.

We all want to succeed in life, to thrive and prosper, and yet we often make inaccurate assumptions about what it really takes to succeed. We presume that success requires us to possess rare

54

talent or have access to money, power, and privilege. We assign success to a unique personality, to luck, or to happenstance—all of which are beyond our control. And by assuming that this is how it works, we inadvertently blind ourselves to opportunities as well as to our own untapped potential.

These assumptions are easy to make and are often reinforced by the collective thinking of those around us. Yet the truth is that many of our nation's most successful entrepreneurs have come from difficult or adverse circumstances. Like Uncle Cleve, they started with little or nothing, yet they chose to respond to their circumstances in a different way and, because they responded differently, they got different results.

Many entrepreneurs have used their adversity to their advantage. Rather than focus on their limitations or blaming their circumstances, they used their hardship as motivation to propel them forward rather than as an excuse that kept them from trying. Instead of engaging in beliefs and behaviors that perpetuated their circumstances, they focused on the future and chose the life they want. Rather than allowing circumstances to dictate their lives, they chose to concentrate their time and energy on things they could change rather than things they could not.

Kinko's founder Paul Orfalea credits his learning disabilities as a blessing that allowed him to see the world differently from his peers. Brian Scudamore started 1-800-GOT-JUNK with $700.00 and a used pickup truck. Jason started his construction site cleaning business with less than $100.

Like Uncle Cleve, these entrepreneurs were open minded about their world and willing to challenge popular wisdom and commonly held beliefs. They often had less to lose—and were therefore in a better position to tolerate risk and uncertainty. And because of the various situations of adversity they found themselves in, they were often more motivated and willing to work longer and harder to achieve their goals.

Clifton Taulbert and Gary Schoeniger

It is this willingness to challenge assumptions and reexamine old ideas that enables entrepreneurs to recognize opportunities that others overlook. It requires a subtle shift in our perspective, one that begins when we ask "what if?" rather than simply mirroring or declaring "what is." It is a tiny shift that enables us to focus on solutions rather than dwelling on problems.

Perhaps the greatest lesson Uncle Cleve left behind is that it is the choices we make that ultimately determine the outcome of our lives.

We all have a need to fit in and a tendency to prefer to follow the crowd. But if we do what we have always done, we will likely get what we have always gotten. As an entrepreneur, it is essential to be conscious of our decisions. We must be willing to rethink old ideas and challenge old assumptions. We must be willing to test the limits of our current beliefs and ideas about who we are and what we are capable of. Rather than accepting limitations, we must be willing to re-imagine our world and reinvent ourselves. We must be willing, as Thoreau suggests, to create the life we imagine.

Our efforts can only take us as far as our knowledge and understanding of the world around us. As an entrepreneur, it is essential to live consciously and to exercise our ability to make conscious choices about how we respond to our circumstances and what we want to have happen in our lives.

This is an ability that can enable you to transform any set of circumstances into a success.

Often, the greatest barriers to success—the greatest obstacles we must overcome—are our own internal beliefs about who we are and what we are truly capable of. The ability to choose enables us to reexamine old ideas and challenge our assumptions—assumptions not just about our own abilities but also about the world around us. It is a shift in our perspective that begins to open our world to new possibilities as well as to our own untapped potential. Ultimately it is a choice—one that can alter the course of our lives.

As Uncle Cleve clearly demonstrated, it is not the lack of money, talent, or education that prevents us from prospering. It is not our circumstances that determine the outcome of our lives. Perhaps the greatest lesson Uncle Cleve left behind is that it is the choices we make that ultimately determine the outcome of our lives.

CHAPTER 2

OPPORTUNITY

"In the midst of difficulty lies opportunity."
—ALBERT EINSTEIN

"Remember, daylight always follows nighttime."
—UNCLE CLEVE

CLIFTON'S ICE HOUSE MEMORIES

Long before I left for St. Louis, I was being prepared to look beyond the challenges and to find the opportunities that were often hidden within problems. At the time, I didn't view Uncle Cleve's ownership of the Ice House as a solution to a problem. I simply saw it as a good business for him and a great job for me. Looking back, I now know that at some point along the way, before his business materialized, an opportunity existed within a problem. Everybody needed ice. The heat in the delta was overwhelming and the humidity was everywhere. Without ice for cold water and to keep food from spoiling, life would have been unbearable.

Clifton Taulbert and Gary Schoeniger

Let me take you back to Glen Allan and to the Ice House when I had no idea that St. Louis, Missouri, would be in my future or even that Uncle Cleve would hire me. Let me take you back to this simple man and his business of providing ice to our community. It sounds rather simplistic today, selling ice, but in his day, he had both solved a major problem and captured a market. Everybody needed ice and yet there were no ice plants in Glen Allan. It was just a small cotton community on Lake Washington that served as a central market area for the surrounding plantations. But people lived there, and to not have access to ice was a major problem. It would have been too difficult for individuals to travel back and forth on a daily basis—sometimes twice daily—to Hollandale, Mississippi, some twenty or so miles away, to get it. Besides, personal transportation was not commonplace like it is today. Cars were a luxury item. I can only remember a very few people having cars in our neighborhoods. But the heat was *real*—and it was everywhere.

The benefits of ice, however, were not a luxury, but a necessity. It was into that world that Uncle Cleve inserted himself as a small business owner. No one is still alive who can tell me the story of how he happened to become the owner of the Ice House or what challenges he faced in obtaining this near monopoly. I just know that by the time I was old enough to understand the life around me, Uncle Cleve was selling ice throughout our community. Not only was he selling and delivering to grocery stores and juke joints, but he also sold from his Ice House porch, making it available to the many field trucks that would need ice for their field hands. He was also delivering ice to the sharecroppers who lived on the surrounding plantations, making it easy for them also to have ice in their homes. If you didn't have a car to come to his Ice House, you could still cool your water, keep your meat from spoiling, and make ice cream on the weekends because of Uncle Cleve's home delivery service. All you had to do was leave your front door open and set out a small handwritten note as to how much ice you wanted delivered that day.

I still remember my first day when we delivered ice to one of the homes in Glen Allan. To prepare for the delivery, we would load the back of the truck with ice, already cut in 25- and 50-pound pieces plus a few 15-pound pieces for those in the community that could only afford a small portion or that had small ice boxes—as rudimentary refrigerators were called back then. With the truck loaded and securely covered with an old green tarp that was big and heavy, I would jump into the cab and try and make room for myself. It was always crowded and stuffed with all the things Uncle Cleve felt he needed— from books to maps, to old worn plaid shirts used to wipe dip sticks and soak up oil spills.

Once securely tucked in, we were off. It felt good being by his side. I could tell from the faces of the people we encountered that we were a welcome sight. He would tip his hat or nod his head, and I would be waving as high and as fast as I could, just like a kid on a parade float. And I could tell when we were getting close to the first house to which ice was to be delivered by the sound of the engine slowing down. Uncle Cleve knew his customers. With the truck stopped, we'd both get out of the cab. We would make our way to the back of the truck where the tarp would be partially removed, just enough to expose a few cuts of ice, but not enough to allow in the blaring sun.

"Cliff, run up there on the porch and git that piece of paper 'tached to that screen door." Without hesitation, I was off and running, opening the gate and hopping up the steps. I grabbed the piece of torn paper that was badly scribbled with just one number: fifteen. I yelled it back to him and watched from the porch as Uncle Cleve pushed the tarp back a bit farther and pulled out the small cut of ice. I watched as he placed the hooks along the sides of the small piece and slowly made his way through the gate, now wide open, to the porch and on into the house. I walked behind him, gawking at all the personal effects I was seeing on the inside, then watched as he walked right to the upright ice box and placed the ice carefully inside. With that delivery made and the front door and gate tightly closed, within a few minutes we were back in the truck and off to the next stop.

He had somehow figured out how not to get on Mr. Walter's field truck.

When I was a kid, my uncle was just selling ice, but now I know that it was so much more. He was being an entrepreneur even though the term was not known within our world. He had somehow figured out how not to get on Mr. Walter's field truck. I have no idea when he first heard the conversation that sparked his interest in filling that much needed void of providing local ice. Nor do I know the counsel that may or may not have been available to him that would support his daring to tackle such a venture at the time he did. I just know he did it. And for a long period of time, his was the only business selling ice in Glen Allan.

UNCLE CLEVE'S MESSAGE

Uncle Cleve was a problem solver. He understood that problems were opportunities and that if he could identify problems and find solutions for other people, he would prosper as well. He did not set out simply to make money for himself. He paid attention to the world around him, staying attuned to problems and issues that others complained about—especially the issues that he could address or improve. He was curious and his mind was constantly engaged, perpetually searching for solutions to the problems of others within his community.

Everyone in Glen Allan needed ice. Uncle Cleve's solutions were not complex; much like delivering coal or wood or fixing cars, these issues did not involve revolutionary new technology or highly specialized knowledge. They did not require large sums of money or access to power and privilege. They were simple solutions to commonplace problems, solutions that were propelled by common sense, solutions rooted in reliability, good service—and a willingness to work long hours and take small risks.

STAIRS TO NOWHERE

Uncle Cleve's lessons continued to shape my young life while I was getting started in St. Louis, a big city that was a far cry from everything I had ever known. There will be more about St. Louis later, but for now, it's important to understand the far-reaching impact of how a problem for one person becomes an *opportunity* for another and how being at the Ice House shifted my perspective of what I expected of myself. This was not just immediately after leaving Glen Allan in 1963; it also applies to a lesson I learned that took place some 23 years later. Uncle Cleve's entrepreneurial mindset had taken hold of my imagination for my own future.

I can still see us in the cab of his truck, driving slowly and talking. "Uncle Cleve, I hear that the white folks are talkin' 'bout how you ended up with the Ice House. How did you?"

"It took some doin'. It wasn't easy. But you see, boy, I always looked to the future, to better myself. Didn't matter that I was 'colored,' I was always talking inside my own head.

63

I always wanted to own something that nobody could take from me. Sharecroppin' is hard work, but they can take it all way from you with one lying bill o' goods. I done saw it over and over. I wanted my own. Like I tole you, if I had yore book learnin', I coulda—well, no use goin' there. I had to use ever bit of thankin' I could muster. I did. I jus' kept putting stuff in my head ever chance I got. When I heard 'bout the Ice House bein' up for sale, I told Mae, this is for us. We put what we had together and we ended up wid it. Thas all."

Such heartfelt conversations would continue to nourish my thoughts and, over time, leave me with the notion that I could be successful in spite of whatever the broader society was saying. Maybe I learned the importance of talking in my "own" head about my "own" future. I learned at an early age to keep my ears and eyes opened for opportunity. I wasn't expecting a registered letter with my name on it and the opportunity inside, but I did know that seeking the best for myself was within my control.

So let's skip ahead to the time I was living in Tulsa, Oklahoma, employed by a local bank, when a business related problem, totally out of my comfort zone, and not bank related, came to my attention. It was a hot day and "somebody needed ice" meaning, that it was an opportunity.

A young startup company which had gone bust during the oil downturn in the eighties had decided to go into the fitness business. With no promise of a quick recovery in the oil field business, they set out to develop a fitness product that was a stationary stair-climbing machine to raise your heart rate and burn calories to help you lose weight. No such thing had ever existed, and the funding institutions did not get it. By the time I heard about this business, they were near bankruptcy with little chance of local much less national success. They had a product, but no one was buying it. At the time, they didn't have a sales team and the rent at their facility was past due. The product was real. The problem was real, and they needed answers fast.

I remember the somber faces around the oblong table where we sat discussing the fate of a then unknown company, simply called Stairmaster. I wasn't intimately familiar with the company. I had read about it in the local Tulsa newspaper which had run articles along with a picture captioned, "Stairs to Where?" At the time no one really understood the application of climbing stairs as beneficial to the heart and general good health. The Stairmaster was an idea brought to life by one man who had a gut feeling that if walking up stairs to an apartment, day after day and week after week, could produce beneficial results in his overall health and physical endurance, then maybe there could be a way to apply this idea, to create a product for others. That lead to the birth of what we know now worldwide as the Stairmaster Exercise System.

In fact, I had no in-depth knowledge of the fitness industry and none about their unique product.

So rather than join the chorus of naysayers (and there were many), I began to think of what I could do to solve the problem. I was totally inspired by this team's commitment to their product and their vision. But I had no money to bring to the table. In most cases, the lack of money can leave you on the outside of the game. In fact, I had no in-depth knowledge of the fitness industry and none about their unique product. That alone would have been reason to walk

Clifton Taulbert and Gary Schoeniger

on by. I couldn't just walk away though. I actually saw myself being an answer to their problem. The problem had grabbed my attention. The product had intrigued me. The product was revolutionary at the time. But it had also become joked about in the media, and without cash or a market, it appeared that there was no real future for a mechanical stairway to nowhere.

As a young black man without money to invest and without product knowledge, all I had to offer was my intuition—a gut feeling that somehow I could make a difference. I was gainfully employed, but I was always reaching up for the next rung on the ladder. Once I had left the cotton fields, I had no desire to ever return again. I was ready to sell ice! I wanted to develop something of my own. I wanted ownership!

Once I had left the cotton fields, I had
no desire to ever return again.

However, that day around that oblong table, all that existed were problems. I remember just sitting and listening and realizing just how bad their situation had gotten. They were up against fitness giants like Nautilus who, at that time, were just laughing at them. Stairmaster had no scientific data to back up their heart- and health-related claims. They were in debt and it seemed that the public could not grasp the potential impact of their product. They needed money to sell some machines, and soon, or their dream would go nowhere. However, in spite of all the negativity, I was impressed by their extreme and unfailing faith in the usefulness of their product. They were determined to succeed, but at that moment in their history seemed to have no solid direction of how to accomplish their goals.

Somewhere between my first introduction to the company and several weeks later, I found myself even more intrigued with their product and the potential of my involvement—even after seeing the rudimentary first product they had produced. The first Stairmaster was hardly related to the sleek machine that we see today. It was bulky. The black oxidized metal was not much to look at, and there were none of the bells and whistles we see today. But the stairs were there and they moved. The company had a problem. I saw an opportunity. I wasn't sure how to flesh out that opportunity at the time, but my commitment was growing stronger each day.

Almost before I knew what I was getting into, my commitment and belief led to a contractual relationship between Stairmaster and me. I secured the rights—or the license—to sell this unknown product to government markets worldwide. Why governments? Because I figured that governments run armies and other security-related entities and their personnel had to stay in shape. Plus, I knew all about the military, having been in the Air Force, or so my thinking was. Opportunity and potential customers, right? Without having ever sold anything to the government before, I just assumed that it would be a piece of cake.

Well, it wasn't. Weeks after obtaining the license, I had not made one sale. And I was getting nowhere fast. Finally, through reading and cold calling, I learned about the National Parks and Recreation Show where many exercise items would be introduced to the government market. Fortunately, the next big show was being held in Kansas City, within driving distance of my Tulsa home. With no prototype to show and only four-color brochures and some product information to help me, my wife and I were off to Kansas, where I expected every buyer there to embrace our product and order it on the spot. I thought the four-color brochures would make it happen.

Clifton Taulbert and Gary Schoeniger

While in Kansas, I realized just how much I didn't know. I was no match for the well-groomed guys from Nautilus and other famous fitness companies. They had booths—slick booths, with even slicker people working them. Potential customers were being given demonstrations. I was way out of my league. But I kept going. I kept talking to anyone who would talk with me. The four-color brochure was not working since most people glanced at it but did not even take it from my hand. Just when I thought it could not possibly get worse, there was another roadblock: the bureaucracy and complexity of the government's purchasing system, the GSA (General Services Administration) and the role that NAF (Non-Appropriated Funds) played in it. I was stunned. And how had I learned about the GSA? Someone took pity on me—that's how! He must have been moved by something I had said, for he was one of the few people at the conference to give me the time of day. I will never forget him. He was a high-ranking non-commissioned officer from the Memphis Air Naval Station, very tall and sported a slightly balding military buzz haircut. He pulled me aside and sat me down in the corner of the auditorium.

I was way out of my league.
But I kept going.

"You may have something here, but you're going about selling it all wrong. You got to have either a NAF or GSA contract. That's how we buy our stuff. People have got to see it as well. It looks like it has potential, but who knows yet? Now if you get yourself a GSA contract, I can talk to you."

*And remember, I was doing all
this while I still had my day job
at the bank.*

I was left speechless. What would be my next step? Who
were these GSA and NAF heads? Where did they live? From
this kind gentleman, I learned that I had to go to Fort Worth,
Texas, to meet them. And you couldn't just walk in and talk.
You had to identify the right buyers and make an appointment
with the purchasing person in charge of that particular item. So
off to Fort Worth I went. And when I left Fort Worth, I had a
stack of papers to fill out that reached practically to the ceiling.
I had no choice but to tackle that mountain of paperwork. And
remember, I was doing all this while I still had my day job at
the bank. This became my night and weekend job. I used all of
my vacation time but I didn't care. I was convinced there was
an opportunity for myself and others within that local problem.
Just that small shift in 1958 from field work to the Ice House
had made a huge difference in my thinking. Uncle Cleve's attitude about his place in life had passed along to me. I completed
the mountain of paperwork and sent it back to Fort Worth.

Low and behold I finally obtained a GSA contract! Kudos to
me, right? At the time I thought that contract would cover everything the federal government would need. But my excitement was
quickly extinguished. After visiting several military fitness centers,
I realized that most of them purchased their fitness equipment
through the NAF contracting procedure. The NAF had completely
slipped my mind. I had to start all over again with more paperwork.
So I did. All the while, I was spending money I didn't have, and
feeling the frustration as weeks turned into months and months
into almost two years before I was ready to contact my unofficial
mentor who'd been so kind to me in Kansas City.

Eventually, I sold the first Stairmaster to the Memphis Air Naval Station. However, the journey to that sale and my subsequent success was burdened with mishaps and struggle along the way. I still marvel that the struggling company had agreed to give me a shot at the government market. On the other hand they really had nothing to lose and everything to gain.

During those two years, the company had made its own inroads. Its domestic sales had spurted, and the design had changed. The product was sleeker. It had some bells and whistles, and the staff's faith and additional investment in their product was paying off. My efforts were too. Pretty soon I was selling to government entities across the country. And it surely didn't hurt when Oprah decided to introduce the Stairmaster on her show. We were off and running.

Just as I had done many years earlier by delivering ice to homes and helping solve small problems for a tiny community on the Mississippi Delta, this company, at one time facing imminent oblivion, was making a major headway in the world of fitness. I may not have been as savvy as I should have been when I started out, but I was there and committed nonetheless, committed to embracing my gut feeling. I had accomplished something!

THE TIMELESS APPLICATION

Problems are simply opportunities in disguise. This elementary yet powerful concept holds the secret to an entrepreneurial mindset. It holds the keys to creating success, regardless of your circumstances.

And, like the other life lessons Uncle Cleve left behind, this simple understanding, this shift in perspective that can expose a world of opportunities as well as our own untapped potential, is a concept that anyone can apply. It does not require unique abilities or special talent, nor power or privilege.

Solutions are the true currency in the entrepreneur's mindset, the currency that enables them to succeed. Solving problems for other people is the "secret" that enables them to transform any set of circumstances into success. It is a simple "secret" yet it is one that is easy to overlook.

Let's face it, most of us are so busy taking care of our own problems, so preoccupied with managing our day-to-day lives, that it never occurs to us that solving problems for other people may be the solution that can empower us and therefore improve our own lives. It's easy to become so focused on problems that we completely overlook solutions.

Many unwittingly focus their time and energy on things over which they have little or no control. Some have a tendency to complain and blame others for their problems rather than engaging their minds and searching for solutions.

Some unconsciously accept their circumstances as something they cannot change. They get stuck on the problem rather than on overcoming it.

And there is often good reason for this mindset. Many of us find ourselves in circumstances where our opinions are not valued or situations that do not necessarily require problem-solving skills. Too often we've been told to pay attention, follow the rules, and do what we're told. We've been informed that those at the top will make all the decisions, and we are expected to toe the line.

We're asked to adhere to narrowly defined job descriptions that focus on repetition and efficiency, leaving little room for innovation and initiative. And, sadly, when we come to believe that our efforts and our ideas don't matter or won't make a difference, we stop having them. We often stop trying. Our ability to solve problems, like a muscle, becomes atrophied—it lies dormant. We never really know what we are capable of because we never try.

Clifton Taulbert and Gary Schoeniger

Yet, while many remain focused on problems, the entrepreneurial mind is searching for a solution. This is a fundamental concept, a shift in awareness that holds the key to accessing a different mindset. It is a fundamental concept that must be understood and embraced.

Some believe that a good "idea" is all they need—like a winning lottery ticket—an "Aha!" moment that holds the key to their success. They set out in search of a great concept that has never been introduced before, yet by doing so, they often overlook opportunities that are right in front of them, opportunities they are unable to see.

Others have an inside-out perspective. Rather than identifying problems and finding solutions for other people, they set out to solve a problem for themselves and hope that others will buy in to their solutions. They mistakenly believe that "if you do what you love, the money will follow," and they strike out on their own. They mistakenly believe that entrepreneurs are gamblers, so they often take unnecessary risks that lead to financial disaster.

Entrepreneurship is not rocket science. It involves risk, yet it is not about gambling. It involves following an idea or a vision, but it is not a mindless dream. Entrepreneurship does not require a genius IQ, specialized knowledge, or technical skills. There is no magic. An entrepreneurial mindset is simply focused on solutions. The world is full of problems, and the solutions are often simple, solutions that do not require specialized knowledge or new technology. They are solutions that do not require access to large sums of money, or an advanced degree. They are simple solutions to everyday problems.

The secret to an entrepreneur's ability to recognize opportunities requires awareness: the willingness to pay attention to what other people need. This problem solving skill is essential to an entrepreneur's ability to recognize opportunity, and it is also a skill that you will need along the way. As an *entrepreneur, you will face challenges on a daily basis—challenges that require creative solutions, challenges that must be overcome in order to proceed.*

Like all other mindset lessons Uncle Cleve passed along, problem solving is a skill that anyone can apply and, like a muscle, it is a skill that can be developed. The more we exercise our problem solving abilities, the better at it we will become.

Look around. What problems can you see? What products or services can you improve? How can you solve those problems? How many people have this problem? How will you let them know about your solution? Will they pay for your solution? These are essential questions that provide insight to the entrepreneurial mindset and the ability to recognize the opportunities that exist within any set of circumstances.

The secret to identifying opportunities simply lies in our ability to be observant, to pay attention to what people need, and to find solutions. This idea is the essence of an entrepreneurial mindset. It is the basic concept that Uncle Cleve understood. Find a problem, and then find a solution. If you can find more people who have the same problem, you can empower yourself.

Clifton Taulbert and Gary Schoeniger

CHAPTER 3

ACTION

"Do not wait; the time will never be right. Start where you stand, and work with whatever tools you may have at your command. . . ."
—NAPOLEON HILL

"Yessir, if you ain't got nothin' planted, ain't nothin' gonna show up."
—UNCLE CLEVE

CLIFTON'S ICE HOUSE MEMORIES

Uncle Cleve was never idle. For him, there was hardly ever any down time. He was always looking up at the next rung on the ladder. His satisfaction came in what he was doing, but he always strove to do it better. In our small neighborhood, where everybody knew everybody else, there was always reason to sit back and have a "pick-up" conversation about plans and ideas and what had been overheard while working. Many times, good ideas were tossed around, but the fear of real world limitations set in place so long ago crippled many. They just didn't know how

Clifton Taulbert and Gary Schoeniger

to break through that barrier. The fact of this reality gives me even greater respect for Uncle Cleve and all that he accomplished within his world in the time he lived. As for many of those neighborhood conversations, many loaded with promise, they simply ended up dead on the ground as those who gathered to talk called it a day, and made their way back to their comfort zones.

> *As for many of those neighborhood conversations, many loaded with promise, they simply ended up dead on the ground as those who gathered to talk called it a day, and made their way back to their comfort zones.*

But it was different for Uncle Cleve. Yes, he was a quiet man and barely ever laughed, but he was thoughtful and he was a planner. I can remember on weekend days going by to visit him. I'd find him sitting in his comfortable chair, an old scratch pad and lead pencil on the floor, his pipe in hand, just leaning back quietly and saying little. He was thinking. He knew I was there. I'd sit across from him and wait for his cough. That was the sign he was ready to smoke his pipe and talk.

"Well boy, been here long?"

"No sir," I'd answer as I watched him write something down on the paper and then sit up straight, cough again, and use a matchstick to dig around in the bowl of his pipe. Once he discovered a few sparks, he would puff and draw air and puff some more. I knew when those efforts were finally successful that his dark face would light up and he would start talking.

"I's jes thinkin' 'bout next week and gittin' it all lined out in my head. Gotta do it with a clear mind if you gonna stay 'head. If it's too much fer yore head to hold, write it down."

Planning and thinking are qualities that are necessary if you are to make things happen as Uncle Cleve did. With some degree of success under his belt, you would think that he'd be content to curb his natural ambition, but not so. He wasn't afraid to take a chance on his ideas, no matter how challenging the process. His ownership of the Ice House was not his stopping place. It only served to spur him on to bigger things.

I can still see the garage he built to work on expensive cars. It had all started with a conversation, one he mulled over in his head and occasionally talked about out loud. When asked, he wasn't afraid to talk about what was on his mind. Oftentimes those "on-his-mind" conversations would take place at Miss Florence and Mr. Isaiah's small neighborhood store. Like him, they were business owners and were among the few adults who had broken with workplace tradition, and hadn't become field workers. The difference, though, was that their small corner store only served people within our "colored" neighborhood, whereas Uncle Cleve's Ice House served the entire community and beyond. There was no segregation at the Ice House.

Often, when at the store for my mother, some of the men, all around his age, who were nearly always playing dominoes in the back half of the small store when not working the fields, would see my appearance as a chance to express themselves about Uncle Cleve and whatever new project he was planning and executing. It would give them the opportunity to yell at me. They just had to say something. So between making strategic moves and taking a swig from their beers, their voices could be heard all the way up front while I waited on my order to be filled.

> *Uncle Cleve's Ice House served*
> *the entire community and beyond.*
> *There was no segregation at the*
> *Ice House.*

"Hey boy, what you and Cleve up to now? He buildin' that garage by night! Totin' wood and sawin' planks. I swear that man never sleeps!"

"God gave everbody 24 hours to git thangs done, but I swear, Cleve done found about five more."

"I bet he done taught you how to drive under the speed limit. That man is sumpin' else."

"Now who's gonna brang them high-dollar cars up in here for him to work on?"

"I tell you that Cleve Mormon just won't let well enough alone. You gonna be just like 'im. We can see that plain as the nose on our face."

I was just a kid, but I had already become associated with Uncle Cleve, his work ethic, and his expectations of himself. At some level, I want to think that they were proud of his ambitious attitude, but in their candor, they simply wanted him to be careful in venturing out so far beyond what had become an acceptable way of life. I can only imagine that many of Uncle Cleve's peers would have tried to talk him out of this latest garage endeavor given the chance. To them it probably made little sense for him to keep stretching beyond his already unusual success. Obviously, neither negative conversations, nor genuine concern, nor perhaps even self-doubt were able to quell Uncle Cleve's enthusiasm or quash his plans. Somewhere along the way, he saw the opportunity, mulled it over in his head, shared a few conversations, and then stepped out to seize it.

He had a natural knack for fixing cars, but that alone would not be enough to build a garage. After ascertaining that a need existed—one that he probably heard about repeatedly while delivering ice along his plantation route—he trusted his gut feeling. This endeavor would require advanced mechanical knowledge that he did not possess. That didn't deter him. On top of all that, he didn't own a "high-dollar" car or truck. That didn't stop him either. He bought a lot and, in his spare time, built the garage. Unknown to many of us, along the way, he secured the mechanic's manuals needed to augment what he had already learned about cars on his own over the years.

Somewhere along the way, he saw the opportunity, mulled it over in his head, shared a few conversations, and then stepped out to seize it.

After his garage was finished, on many Saturday afternoons, after my chores for Ma Ponk were done or schoolwork completed, I would walk down to the garage and there would be my boss . . . now functioning as a high-dollar car mechanic. Dressed in overalls, he'd be nearly all the way under a Packard, twisting and turning nuts and bolts and sliding out from under the car every so often to look at a manual that was lying open by his side. Unlike so many others at the time, his conversation had turned into reality, not just for him, but also for the many folk who would subscribe to his ice delivery service and then bring their cars to his high-end mechanic's garage.

79

Uncle Cleve was dedicated to his own success. Although he built and ran his garage, the Ice House remained his primary business, the place where he remained unafraid of taking action to realize his dreams—regardless of whether they might have seemed impossible or impractical. This was the way of life for Uncle Cleve and it was happening right in front of me. We were always working. And he was always defying the status quo by his actions.

For him, my age was never an issue. When something needed to be done, I was pulled right into the action. Uncle Cleve left me with the understanding that there were very few things that I could not do, even though the world was telling me differently. To Uncle Cleve, nothing was more important than right now. He didn't mind me taking a break, so long as it did not interfere with work.

"Hey Cliff, boy we ain't got all day. We gotta git the ice lined up 'long side the wall. You git it done now, then you don't lose no time when we git ready to unload the new ice. You can rest when the work is done."

He was lifting ice as he called me to action. He was not one to talk and talk and talk and finally talk himself out of the action required. He was a man of action, which was evident in all that he did, whether it was running his Ice House or fixing expensive cars or buying up additional property with his profits, as he eventually did. He never cursed the energy he had to expend to get his work done, just sweated and smiled that slight grin that never quite broke out across his entire face. And soon, this man who started out with so little and had so much going against him, became a car collector too, which at the time was unheard of within our neighborhood. That was Uncle Cleve.

UNCLE CLEVE'S MESSAGE

Uncle Cleve was a man of action. He was always in motion, and his mind was always fully engaged. Once he had identified an opportunity and gathered the information he needed, he set his plan into motion. He was not one to make excuses, and he was not afraid to try something new. Although he had no formal education, he was not afraid to learn. He acted on his ideas and gave little credence to what others thought of him. He focused his precious time and energy on things he could change.

And work was not his enemy. Rather than approaching work as an unpleasant experience, it was something he took pride in; something he enjoyed. In spite of the circumstances that surrounded him and the limitations that were beyond his control, he chose to focus on those things that he could change. He understood the power of his actions and fully embraced the qualities of the entrepreneurial mindset.

UNDER INVESTIGATION

Now let me take you back to a time prior to Stairmaster that illustrates the effects of Uncle Cleve's influence way beyond Glen Allan. This is what is so amazing about the gift he gave me of a mindset based on action—it could stay within me no matter what the endeavor. It all may have started in 1958 when I was just about 13, but his influence had crept into my way of thinking and stayed with me. I knew I could do more than sit in the back of a store and play dominoes. I knew I, too, could build a garage for high-dollar cars if that's what my gut was telling me to do.

Clifton Taulbert and Gary Schoeniger

Well, I was reminded of that lesson while I was in the Air Force during the end of the Vietnam War. I had already completed basic training at Lackland Air Force Base and had been assigned to Dow AFB in Bangor, Maine, until we shipped out to Vietnam. It was a scary time for young airmen. I worked in our squadron's headquarters and was very familiar with the orders for Vietnam that were coming in daily both for draftees as well as enlisted men. My friends were leaving, and many of them would return in body bags. Was this my unavoidable lot in life?

One day at the barracks, I had this gut feeling to canvass the barrack's bulletin board. This made very little sense in that most of what was on our bulletin board came out of the office where I worked. But I followed my instinct. While I was at the board, guys would pass by and comment. When off-duty, I was simply called "Professor." That's the way life was in the military. We went out of our way to create our own culture, even giving each other special names, some that were carried beyond your enlistment and some that were forgotten as soon as you received your discharge orders.

"Hey, Professor, whatchu lookin' for? Your orders to 'nam?"

"Professor, you gonna hit the town with us tonight?"

That day I just laughed them off and kept perusing, peeling back ancient notices and even older news. Finally, I saw a small newspaper clipping stuck on the board with a stickpin. I had to really adjust my eyes to read it. The print was that small. Someone had clipped out an article about an opening in the 89th Presidential Wing at Andrews AFB in Washington, D.C. Peering at the article, I felt like I was eavesdropping on a conversation that perhaps was not meant for me, just like Uncle Cleve no doubt had overheard the need for a fancy auto repair garage many years earlier. But that didn't stop him. He saw a chance and he took it.

82

So I took the clipping down and back to my room with me, where I read it over and over and over. I realized that to apply for this job was the longest shot I had ever taken in my life. Was the opportunity even still available? With the memory of segregated Mississippi still in my head, I felt sure that this position was being reserved for a white airman—even though the clipping clearly said it was open to all. Would they even consider me? I was torn between anticipation and fear.

Looking for support later that night, I told one of my roommates, Robuck, that I was thinking about applying for this job, one that could not only change my life, but also possibly even save it. For me it would be the opportunity of my military lifetime, a high-profile position in the nation's capitol. I couldn't believe I had the courage to even think that I could compete for this opportunity. I had not gone to college, and my high school diploma was from the ultra-secluded delta of Mississippi.

Would they even consider me? I was torn between anticipation and fear.

I wanted Robuck to say, "Hey man, go for it!" But Robuck was little help. He just flat out told me that I would never get such a plum assignment and with a few choice comments, went back to sleep. From his perspective, an assignment to Vietnam was in my future, not a top-secret job in Washington, D.C. that would require a background check and security clearance. That's just the way he was. Follow the system and go with the flow.

But I wanted more. I had learned that I didn't have to pick cotton just because everyone else did. I wanted this opportunity in spite of what my roommate had said. No doubt thousands of airmen would be applying for that position.

Clifton Taulbert and Gary Schoeniger

I carried the crumpled newspaper clipping around for several more days, when finally, I realized that if I didn't get my application in the hopper before the deadline, nothing was going to happen, no matter how I felt. I would be sent to Vietnam, that was for sure. At some point, I had to come to the realization that my fate was not in the hands of my roommate. My fate was in my hands. It was up to me to take the required action, no one else but me. If I failed, then I failed, but at least I would have tried.

So I did what I had to do. I wrote the required letter responding to what was asked of the applicant and quietly dropped it into the mailbag where I worked. It was done. I had taken the first step necessary to change my fate. After several weeks, I forgot about it. I never mentioned my application to anyone else, and I went about my work.

Then one day, I got a letter from the FBI. I was afraid to open it. I wasn't sure what it would say. Was I in some kind of trouble? What on earth had I done to get a letter from the FBI? I never associated it with the application. When I finally opened it and devoured the contents, I realized that while I was waiting for the job at the 89th and then forgetting to wait anymore, FBI agents had gone back to Glen Allan to do a thorough background check. I can only imagine the stir it evoked in that small cotton community. They had also traveled to St. Louis, where I had lived and worked, and talked with people who had known me there. With the background investigation complete, the military somehow came to the conclusion that I was the one.

Had I not taken the personal action required—even though the goal seemed insurmountable, my chances nil—I never would have been the one selected for that assignment. Being around Uncle Cleve was like having a gift that kept on giving. Just as he had acted by building the garage of his dreams,

I had also acted on my gut feeling. I had built my garage! With Robuck and my other friends congratulating me and wishing me well, I packed my duffel bag to join the 89th Presidential Wing at Andrews Air Force Base near the nation's capitol in Washington, D.C.

THE TIMELESS APPLICATION

Becoming an entrepreneur is a dream for millions of people throughout the world. It is a dream that inspires hope and offers the chance to reach for a better life. It is a common dream that reaches across continents and across all social and economic boundaries. It is a dream that dwells in the heart as well as in the mind.

And, as Uncle Cleve showed, becoming an entrepreneur is a dream we can all aspire to. All it requires is taking action.

Entrepreneurs are action oriented. Like Uncle Cleve, they are internally driven, and they clearly understand the power of effort applied to knowledge and new ideas. They view their time as currency—and they spend it well. They do not waste time and energy on things over which they have no control. And they won't complain about a problem without also considering a solution.

Rather than blaming others or allowing circumstances to dictate their lives, they are willing to test their ideas. They tend to concentrate their efforts on things they can change.

Entrepreneurs also understand that if they do what they have always done, they will get what they have always gotten.

And while this may seem like an obvious truth, when it comes to taking action, this is where many get stuck. A closer look may help us understand why.

85

We all have hopes and dreams. We all want to reach for a better life. We all have a desire to participate, to have our ideas implemented and to make a difference in the world. Yet we often fall prey to a self-limiting mindset, and we never really try. Without realizing it, we adopt beliefs and make assumptions that are at odds with our own self-interests.

Some may talk about their ideas or things they intend to do. Some make excuses and focus on things they cannot change. Others simply complain.

Some lack the confidence in their own abilities and are afraid to try. Some are convinced that the barriers to entry are too high, so they never bother to try.

Without realizing it, many become externally driven, reacting to their circumstances rather than choosing their response. Without realizing it, they focus on things around them they cannot change while completely overlooking or ignoring the things they can. And when they do, they unwittingly render themselves powerless. Their untapped potential lies dormant because they never try.

Some mistakenly believe that a "good idea" holds the secret to their success. They imagine that simply coming up with that good idea will solve all their problems and make their dreams come true. They search randomly for the "Aha!" moment, the big idea that often never comes. Meanwhile, they often overlook opportunities that are right within their reach.

The truth is that good ideas are a commodity, but taking action is what really counts. In fact, many of today's most successful companies were founded on a simple concept and started by entrepreneurs like Uncle Cleve—people equipped with very few resources that nevertheless understood the power of action and were not afraid to try.

For most, it's not the lack of money, luck, or talent that prevents us from prospering. It's not the external barriers that deny our hopes and dreams. For many it is the internal barriers, the self-imposed limitations that must be overcome in order to succeed.

Like an invisible fence, many of us have invisible barriers, self-imposed limitations that are buried deep within our minds. We make assumptions about the world around us, about who we are and what we're capable of. By making these assumptions and accepting them to be true, we shut ourselves off from a world of possibilities. Sadly, we never know what we are capable of simply because we never try.

Albert Einstein once defined insanity as doing the same thing over and over while expecting different results.

Entrepreneurs embrace change. They understand the connection between knowledge, effort, and reward and they are willing to put themselves out there. Simply put, they are willing to try.

An entrepreneurial mindset requires us to be willing to push the limits of what we think we are capable of, to take personal risks, and to take action—action that often forces us to leave the confines of our comfort zone and to explore the boundaries of our own self-imposed limitations.

As Uncle Cleve would surely tell you, becoming an entrepreneur requires us to think for ourselves, to challenge old ideas, and to reexamine our assumptions. It necessitates our paying attention to the world around us, looking for problems and finding solutions. It requires us to focus on things we can change. It requires us to reinvent ourselves. And it all starts with taking action.

Clifton Taulbert and Gary Schoeniger

CHAPTER 4

KNOWLEDGE

"Be observing constantly. Stay open minded.
Be eager to learn and improve."
—JOHN WOODEN

"Mix 'em up, boy: hard work and book learnin'."
—UNCLE CLEVE

CLIFTON'S ICE HOUSE MEMORIES

In Glen Allan in the 1950s, where life was bound by tradition and supported by the weight of the prevailing law, an African American who showed curiosity about life and searched for knowledge could have put himself in real trouble. There were no signs on any corner encouraging Uncle Cleve and his peers to seek knowledge. In fact, it was just the opposite. Those "colored boys" were needed for their muscles not their brains. This had been the tradition in the south for so long that many people, through time and circumstance, bought into that system. And that system did not make space for

89

most black people to pursue knowledge. Uncle Cleve was among the few who ignored that system. He broke open his own space and sought knowledge in the opportunities he created for himself. In doing so, Uncle Cleve silently—but actively—demonstrated his own value and brought value into the lives of others. For the most part, entrepreneurs in those days had to become their own cheerleaders—often with nary a shout or a peep. Uncle Cleve did it that quiet way. I saw the value of doing it that way as well.

Without much formal education to recommend him and with the tools he had available to him, he embarked on a journey of learning how to realize his goal and then put that knowledge into action.

While working for Uncle Cleve, I saw him buck the system as he wholeheartedly embraced the quest for whatever knowledge he needed to enlarge his world beyond the confines of small minds. As his world grew, so did his quest for more. Without much formal education to recommend him and with the tools he had available to him, he embarked on a journey of learning how to realize his goal and then put that knowledge into action. This pattern remained part of his life for as long as he was alive. His lack of formal education did not hamper him in his continued quest to learn more and to do more. It set him apart within our community, garnered him its respect, and spurred him on to successfully accomplish many endeavors. It seemed that the more he learned, the more he wanted to do. And the more he did, the more he wanted to learn. This circle of learning and becoming was not lost on me.

This was the world Uncle Cleve invited me to join in 1958. I was privileged to work with him during those hot summer months. The Ice House became my college. Yes, I cut and delivered ice instead of reading great literature. But the cab of his truck and the porch of his Ice House were my classrooms. I saw how Uncle Cleve maneuvered his life around the boundaries of our segregated system, never failing to have high expectations for himself. I learned lessons I would never forget.

In a world and during a time where physical prowess defined a man, Uncle Cleve talked about education and learning. He came right out and said they meant a lot to him.

The Ice House became my college.

"I wuz deliverin' ice the other day to Mr. Jake's store, and I saw this old man from the Colony trying to make his 'X' on his bill. It was so sad. Rumor 'round here's that he kin pick over seven hunerd pounds o' cotton a day, but he cain't write out his own name. I 'spect it ain't his doing. Boy, git yore education. Fill your head up with stuff. Miss Maxey and them down at the 'colored' school is doing a mighty fine job, but y'all gotta stick wid it. I'm so glad I don't hafta mark me no X."

Such conversations would usually start while we were busy at work, but would always end up being finished in the cab of his truck while he was taking me home. Sitting in the cab, I was held captive by Uncle Cleve's wisdom. He was never pompous, nor was he a braggart. He just wanted me to know that this was my day, and I had to make the best of the time allotted me. Most of the men in our neighborhood never

91

seemed to have the time for meaningful conversation. Uncle Cleve was different. He relished the opportunity to share what he had learned, and what better place to do that than the cab of his truck? I was a captive, a happy young man who hung on to his every word while he drove slowly down the many unpaved roads in the delta. I recall no cool breeze to refresh us or alleviate the hot re-circulated air of the engine and the smell of our salt and sweat. But there I sat, sucking in my boss's unusual take on life, which nearly always started out with him saying,

"Now, boy . . . like I was sayin'." When I heard those words, I knew what was next: I was in class.

"Like I was sayin' back at the Ice House—when you almos' dropped that 50-pound piece of ice on my foot?—man is smart." This was his oft-repeated rhetorical beginning: mankind is smart. "Change is gonna come. I kin see it all around me. We cain't do this o' type work forever. You gotta be prepared. You gotta fill up your head 'fore the future slips in on you, you know."

Uncle Cleve knew the value of "getting stuff in your head"—as he called formal learning. He had a continuous quest for knowledge. Learning had worked for him. And he believed it always would.

On those hot summer days, as we slowly made our way home, I just listened as he talked, prodded, and asked questions. "Boy, 'member what I done tole you the other day? How you doing in the books?" Before I could answer him, Uncle Cleve was on to the next comment. "You gotta get stuff in your head. It ain't like it used to be. You need to mix 'em up: hard work an' book learnin'. Yes sirree-bob, sho' gonna need your head learnin'. Now you take yore cousin, my boy Joe, he was a hard worker; but he finished the school over there at Hollandale with 'fessor Simmons. I made sho he stayed in school. 'fessor Simmons and them is all over there in Hollandale where I get ice, you know. Joe wanted to lay 'bout like some o' the others 'round here, but I wouldna hear of it. Now he's in the service, cross the waters somewhere, and making good o' hisself. Yeah, he'll be alright. You gotta do that—fill up yore head."

Also during our slow rides through Glen Allan or out among the plantations, I picked up on the importance of observation and listening as learning tools. Uncle Cleve had much to say about business, but unfortunately, his color kept him from having those significant conversations with his peers from the other side of the tracks. However, those limitations did not keep him from observing success and finding ways to implement what he had observed in his own life. One person he felt was worthy of his observation was Milton Fried, the Jewish owner of the local hardware and general store. I'd hear all about it while riding with him to deliver ice or pick up ice from the plant in Hollandale.

"Now, boy, you take that Milton Fried. Now that's a solid businessman. He Jewish, you know, but he a good man. You know him, don't you? His people been livin' 'roun' here for some time now."

"Yessir, I do know him. I know his mother also. Sometimes she allows us to pick pecans in her pecan grove. She's a nice lady. One day she invited me and Bobby in for some food."

"Did you'all go in?"

"Yessir, but I was scared at first. She's white, I guess, but we went in anyway and she fed us. I was standing up, but she made us sit down at the table. The food was good."

"Yes, I 'spect it was. I knew her husband 'fore he done passed away. He's a good man. He passed it on to his boy, Milton. Well anyway, with things bein' the way they is down heah, race issues and all, I watched for some time how Milton treats everbody wit' respect—black, white, farmers, day workers, or anybody. I learned a lot watching him over the years. Thas how

Clifton Taulbert and Gary Schoeniger

I run my Ice House, you know. I treat everbody with respect. That way you don't leave nobody out. Folks can't fault you for treating folks right."

Uncle Cleve may not have had an advanced degree in human psychology, but he sure did know how to treat people the right way. He may not have possessed all the traditional tools that might lead to success, but he wasn't afraid, or too stubborn to search them out and put them to use once he figured out how. Mr. Fried probably never knew of his contribution to the Ice House business and to its operational success. Observing Mr. Fried and the way he showed his respect to everybody in our highly stratified community was all the psychology that Uncle Cleve needed.

> *Uncle Cleve may not have had an advanced degree in human psychology, but he sure did know how to treat people the right way.*

Uncle Cleve was also not one to let age distract him. In his middle age, fully aware that he had missed the boat on formal education, it would have been acceptable for him to just muddle along—everybody else in his shoes seemed to. But from the manuals he studied at his garage to the people he observed, there is no doubt that Uncle Cleve knew how seeking knowledge had contributed to his success. Learning wasn't a burden to him; he wanted to learn. He wanted to know what was going on beyond Glen Allan. The cab of his truck was always stuffed with books, manuals, and newspapers. Always. There was never a time I did not have to push them over to find room to sit. It was important to him to have the tools of knowledge alongside him—literally and figuratively.

Uncle Cleve also listened to the radio with a passion: news, music, entertainment shows and weather—it did not matter. All of it held the potential for learning. His mind was not held captive by the cotton fields right outside our doors. He wasn't stuck in the past. And he wasn't totally comfortable with the present. He was future focused. It didn't matter what society was telling him. It mattered what he was telling himself.

And so he passed his use of observation and his practice of learning whenever possible along to me. He wanted me prepared for a world that had already undergone major changes—with even more to come. "Cliff, keep yore eyes open. Git yore books—fill up yore head, but 'member, you can learn a thang or two from some of the folks who will shorely cross yore path. I sho do."

> *It didn't matter what society was telling him. It mattered what he was telling himself.*

Looking back at my teenage self, I know I was being shown how to live beyond limitations and about the importance of seeking knowledge and embracing curiosity. But the choice to do so would be mine. When Uncle Cleve's eyes became too dim to read, his conversations about life and what was going on in the country and the world continued from a comfortable chair with his ever-present pipe lit up and filling the room with a sweet, pungent odor. From him, I realized that there was more to life than Saturday nights at the juke joints. I had to make time to study, to find out what I needed to know if I was to succeed in life. I had to realize that life was a school from which one never graduates. I have followed his example all my life.

Clifton Taulbert and Gary Schoeniger

UNCLE CLEVE'S MESSAGE

Although Uncle Cleve had little formal education, he was a wise man who understood the value of knowledge and was not afraid to learn. He was a curious man, and he understood the power of knowledge and the clear connection between knowledge, effort, and reward.

He developed an insatiable curiosity about the world around him, and for Uncle Cleve, learning became a self-directed, lifelong pursuit. Rather than accepting his lack of formal education as a limitation, he sought knowledge wherever he could find it. Rather than spend his idle time carelessly, he constantly searched for answers, his mind perpetually engaged. An avid reader, he sought knowledge and insight from others. He was an observant man who became a lifelong student as well as a teacher.

He was also open-minded, willing to challenge his own assumptions as well as the commonly held beliefs of those around him.

LUNCH AT THE PLAYBOY CLUB

I'd like to come back now to St. Louis and to the pots and pans room where I worked and then to the new job at the bank that came my way. If you recall, getting that first job in the public cafeteria of the big downtown department store was a real setback to me. Even though I worked hard and thoroughly cleaned the pots and pans, I felt humiliated. But it seemed as if nothing else was coming my way—that is until the job at Jefferson Bank and Trust opened up. At first I was overjoyed. So were my relatives and friends. Imagine that! The boy from the country who had come to the city had gotten that big ole bank job. This excitement would prove to be short lived.

96

My first day at the bank hurled me even further back to the world I thought I had left behind. Being a bank messenger was nothing more than being a glorified porter. I was not in the pots and pans room, but I felt as though I was in the banking equivalent of that hidden back room. When I interviewed with the bank, I'd been told about the St. Louis Federal Reserve and the trips I would make there on a daily basis. Travel was no problem, I had told them that I was ready.

Reality, however, was different. As the job revealed itself, it consisted of little more than the intellectually challenging duty of holding the door open for customers. I'll always remember how I felt while standing there in a uniform like a wooden puppet holding the door open for others. Some would speak to me or acknowledge my existence, but more often, I felt as if I was being looked through—as if I didn't exist. The customers just looked at me as if I was born to stand at that door. They had no idea that I had been born to run the Ice House. My job also included driving the president of the bank, Mr. Dillon Ross, to the Playboy Club, and delivering cancelled checks to the Federal Reserve. I also had to police the bank grounds. In other words, all of my responsibilities were outside that bank. I knew I had to do something to change that picture. I also knew that the people in the inside looking out were not looking out for me. My future was up to me.

It was during one of my breaks, which I was permitted to take inside the bank, that I overheard a conversation about a class being offered at the St. Louis Institute of Banking. It was not presented to me as something I might want to attend, however I saw it as something that might move my career along. So I approached the human resources department to ask about it. I was told that first I had to get through my probation period, and so I did. Then I went back to the office and asked again about the banking class. I knew the value of knowledge and wanted to aim for something beyond the messenger position. It took a while and a lot of persistence. Some of the higher ups—all of whom were white—would talk with me about it, but their responses revolved around how hard the school could be. Then I remembered Uncle Cleve and his urging me to fill up my head. And so I listened to the managers talk but kept requesting I be given that opportunity anyway.

Finally, after a few months, I was given the opportunity. As long as my grades were maintained, the bank would pay my tuition. I remember that first night of class. Yes, I had to go at night, and right after work on some days. It interrupted my leisure time, but as I had learned from Uncle Cleve, there was much more to life than hanging out at juke joints or playing dominoes in my free time. I was thinking about the future. The class was held downtown—a downtown with which I had not yet become familiar. I still remembered Glen Allan and the few graveled roads we had to travel; there were no tall buildings and no elevators back home. St. Louis had changed my world. With no one from the bank to ride with, I finally found the building where the classes were held. I stood outside the door for a while and drew a really deep breath, then I walked in.

Looking around, I saw no one who resembled me. The all-white class stared at me as if I had come from outer space. No one made noticeably negative comments; they just remained quiet. Obviously, they knew all about the Civil Rights marches that had gone on for months to integrate the banks in St. Louis. And in truth I owed my presence in part to that effort. But the rest would be up to me.

With my class books handed to me, I found a seat. Although I was surrounded by people, I felt very much alone. I had no study partners. The material was completely foreign to me. But I knew how to listen and to take good notes. Plus, I was determined to knock that ball out of the park.

Eventually, test time arrived. I was nervous. First, the grades would be sent to the bank's HR contact and then shared with the administration. As much as I wanted to do well, that first test filled me with tension and self-doubt. I kept seeing my classmates and recalling how comfortable they were speaking up when questions were asked. It was much easier for them; they were all already employed at some level of actual banking. I was the only messenger in the class. I was not sure if I could engage at the same level as my peers. For days, I waited for my grades and tortured myself with scenarios of how I would respond when I learned how I had done.

I was the only messenger in the class.

My fears soon proved groundless. My first test score was near perfect—and so were the others that followed. I felt I had to do a good job—for myself, and for those who looked like me. Their chance rested upon my performance. With rumors of my good grades circulating the bank, I wanted more. I wanted a real job on the inside where no confining uniform was required. Every chance I got, I volunteered to help out in the accounting department tallying checks. But no invitation to join the real banking system was forth-coming. I kept asking, but nothing changed. I had good grades, incredibly good grades, but I was still picking up trash and feeling trapped by a time and place where racial segregation relegated black people to menial service positions and colored-only sections.

Curiosity and the drive to push beyond those ridiculous boundaries intervened. I knew I had to change the course of my life. While all of my messengering and door-opening was

99

going on, so was the Vietnam War. I had a rather low draft number, but with my so-called banking job going nowhere, I decided to join the Air Force. I enlisted and resigned from the bank—well before I had an opportunity to offer any true value to the company. I left the bank still a simple messenger.

Within weeks, I was going through basic training at Lackland Air Force Base. Though the military was structured, I was still looking to a better future. I had no idea how this would turn out; I just had to wait and see. All I knew was that I wanted more, that the Air Force offered more opportunity, and I wasn't afraid to work hard to achieve my objective. I realized that I had to factor myself into the mix of my expectations. That was another one of Uncle Cleve's lessons. I had to be able to count on myself.

THE TIMELESS APPLICATION

Curiosity and the pursuit of knowledge are critical aspects to an entrepreneurial mindset. And, like the other mindset lessons, they are skills we can all learn to develop, ones we can all learn to apply.

Knowledge—combined with effort—is the engine that drives entrepreneurs. It is the rocket that thrusts them beyond their limitations, beyond their circumstances, leading them toward their goals. Entrepreneurs are internally driven and understand the power of knowledge. Rather than engage in mindless pastimes, they search constantly for knowledge that can expose new opportunities and empower them to create the life they have imagined.

We often make important choices based on incomplete knowledge and limited expectations. We make choices based on unchallenged assumptions, things we may have been told or assume to be true, yet have never really tested for ourselves. When we do so, we may overlook new opportunities that untap our potential.

As an entrepreneur, it is essential to understand the connection between knowledge, effort, and outcome. After all, our knowledge influences the choices we make. And the choices we make will ultimately determine the outcome of our lives. As we have said elsewhere, if we do what we have always done, we are likely to get what we have always gotten.

Working harder is by itself rarely the answer. Once we become internally driven, we must realize that our efforts can only take us as far as our understanding. Doing more of what we are already doing will rarely produce the outcome we desire. If we are to accomplish our goals, we must increase our knowledge.

This is an essential aspect of an entrepreneurial mindset. Think about it, and embrace it. Because, while this concept may seem simple and self-evident, it is one we often overlook.

For many, there is a disconnect between knowledge, effort, and outcome. Without realizing it, we develop a closed mindset, a mindset that dampens our curiosity and discourages learning. We become blind to new opportunities.

Many engage in behavior that perpetuates their circumstances rather than improving their lives. Some people become convinced that life is a lottery, and that they have been left behind. Like survivors in a lifeboat, they respond to the wind and currents and tide rather than steering for a destination reflecting their own desire. They feel no reason to be curious, to seek knowledge, to look for answers and to learn. Rather than accepting responsibility and reaching for a better life, they passively accept their circumstances. They stop trying.

Some blame others for their circumstances. Rather than seeking knowledge that can help improve their lives, they tend to focus their time and energy blaming others for their

Clifton Taulbert and Gary Schoeniger

disappointments while overlooking opportunities to improve their own lives. Without realizing it, they inadvertently adopt the position of weakness and victim-hood that renders them powerless to change. They become attached to an attitude that is at odds with their own self-interest.

Many of us have been encouraged to follow the rules. We do what we are told. We stick to narrowly defined job descriptions that focus on repetition and efficiency while eliminating the need to be curious and to seek knowledge. Many view education as a one-time event.

Others equate learning with an unpleasant and institutionalized experience that has little or no meaning. They remain disconnected from new ideas and locked out of a brighter future.

Rather than embracing a fixed mindset, entrepreneurs like Uncle Cleve approach life as a series of experiments. They constantly ask themselves "what if?" questions, continually test their ideas and search for solutions. They combine "book learning" with effort and real-world knowledge and experience.

This approach to life is a fundamental aspect of an entrepreneurial mindset. It is a basic principle that enables entrepreneurs to recognize opportunities that others overlook.

In today's world, knowledge is easy to access and readily available. And, rather than view learning as a one-time event or allow others to define their educational limitations, entrepreneurs like Uncle Cleve become self-directed, lifelong learners who seek knowledge in a variety of ways.

Perhaps the greatest source of knowledge comes from experienced entrepreneurs who have been where we intend to go. Entrepreneurs have valuable knowledge and insight gained from their experience that they are often willing to share with others who are willing to listen, and to help those who are also on their way to a life of entrepreneurial success. They are a vital resource not to be overlooked.

Curiosity, like a muscle, can be developed over time. However, if we assume that outside forces are stacked against us and that our efforts will not improve our lives, we lose incentive to be curious. Yet when we understand how knowledge applied to effort can improve our lives, our minds awaken to new possibilities; our curiosity ignites a renewed desire to learn. Since information is easy to obtain, learning can take place anywhere, at any time.

Always looking, always learning, always working. Entrepreneurs approach life as a continuous series of experiments. They are action oriented, and they learn by doing. If they do not get the results they desire, they learn from their mistakes. They make adjustments, and they try again.

Learning to develop an entrepreneurial mindset—like any other skill—takes time. It will require us to do things that are unfamiliar, to address matters we have never considered, to face issues that may seem uncomfortable. It will require us to leave our comfort zones, and set out on an exciting new path—a path toward the life we have imagined.

While at first our efforts may seem awkward, through perseverance and determination, the entrepreneurial mindset will slowly become second nature.

Once we accept that it is our knowledge combined with effort that ultimately determines the outcome of our lives, we become internally driven and accept responsibility for where our life is headed. We become future-focused and begin to make conscious, pro-active choices. Rather than being pounded by winds and current, we begin to set sail for a destination, one that we have chosen rather than one we have unwittingly accepted.

WHO OWNS THE ICE HOUSE? *Eight Life Lessons From An Unlikely Entrepreneur*

CHAPTER 5

WEALTH

"If money is your hope for independence, you will never have it.
The only real security that a man will have in this world is
a reserve of knowledge, experience and ability."
—HENRY FORD

"Boy, some folks spend ever' penny they git and'll borrow to
spend more. You cain't live like that."
—UNCLE CLEVE

CLIFTON'S ICE HOUSE MEMORIES

"**L**ook at Cleve, driving so slow, time has to honk."

For some, my uncle's slow driving was a sign of arrogance—him trying to be different from everybody else. No, he wasn't being arrogant, but he was definitely being different. His quiet and thoughtful approach to life was so completely opposite of what was then the prevailing norm in our small southern neighborhood. He wasn't arrogant, but truth be told,

Clifton Taulbert and Gary Schoeniger

he was not like many of the men I knew. He was his own man who always responded to life from his own perspective, not the perspective that others had defined for him. And it showed up even in his driving. He was not one to do things just to be seen by others. Even when driving, very seldom did he honk his horn or yell from his open window to announce his presence. Instead, he politely tipped his hat or nodded his head, his pipe clenched between his teeth. That was Uncle Cleve—a man on a mission, a man whose message was set by example, or by a quiet command expressed at just the right moment.

Uncle Cleve had a very methodical way of approaching life. He established certain patterns of action and very seldom did they change. From the day I started at the Ice House to the day I left, I knew how our day would go. No matter how hard the work, the day would eventually end with the both of us having put in a good day of work. With the last customer served and the sun sinking into Lake Washington, it was nearly time to call it quits for the day. It was time for me to sweep up. Afterward we'd go into the small, crowded office and count the days' receipts. With the money counted and locked inside the green cash box, I would then tidy the inside of the ice bin by arranging the full and partial blocks of ice to make it easy for the next morning. I knew Uncle Cleve trusted me because he'd call out to me to secure the place.

That was Uncle Cleve—
a man on a mission, a man whose
message was set by example, or by
a quiet command expressed at
just the right moment.

"Cliff, you got them doors padlocked?" I assured him they were and then we were off. "Come on, boy, let's call it a day." As always, I jumped into the cab of the truck and settle in for a talk. With smoke from his pipe circling his head, he would begin class, "Cliff, like I tole you, if you gonna make something outta yore life, you gotta have sumpin' of yore own put away. You don't need everthang yore eyes want."

From him I learned so much. I treasure the lessons he imparted on how to value the role of money in my life and the leverage it provided. Of course, I was just a teenager with literally no money to speak of when those lessons were being taught. Although he was called cheap by many of those who knew him, I never forgot what he told me, especially when I saw how Uncle Cleve would parlay the profits from his business into yet another entrepreneurial pursuit.

---

*You don't need everthang yore
eyes want.*

Money did not flow freely within our neighborhood. Although hard work was commonplace, the financial rewards of the work were less than satisfactory. Few had money beyond what was needed for survival; thus the challenge of understanding how to use it to fund the future was nil. But Uncle Cleve, in spite of the reality that surrounded his life and dictated otherwise, acquired the knowledge of how to save and use money wisely. While working for him, I became privy to conversations that reflected his deep thinking. He was adamant about saving. From his perspective, there was never a reason not to be saving. I recall one day so many years ago when we were sitting together on the front porch of the Ice House.

He was already smoking his pipe and the sweet and tangy smell of Prince Albert Tobacco permeated the air. When he leaned his stocky body back in the cane bottom chair, I was prepared to listen. "Boy, some folks spend every' penny they git and'll borrow to spend more. You cain't live like that, no siree-bob, you cain't live like that. Take my boy, Joe. He's cross the waters now, somewheres in Germany, but I done tole him while he was with me, and I tell you the same thing: if'n you spend it that means somebody else got it. I see you friends 'round here. They git a dime or two and it's like they start setting they hands on fire. They cain't wait to spend it all. That's what the folks want 'em to do. You gotta start young wid the right pattern in your head, boy. You gotta save to have."

At that time in my life, I had not given much thought to saving. I guess I had not given much thought to my future, but Uncle Cleve had my future on his mind. While I was trying to figure out if I had anything to save, Uncle Cleve was clearing his throat. He was on a roll, so I listened as he continued. "You know me and Willie Mae bought some houses a while back."

I wasn't sure if he wanted me to answer him or just listen, but I finally managed to let out a rather mild, "Yessir."

"We had the money all saved up. Look at these shoes on my foot. Same shoes for years. They wear well. I got rubber on the soles. Put it there o'er the hole myself. I got one pair for occasions, but dats all. Too many shoes is more like steppin' on my own money. Mae, she done took on more cookin' jobs than a body in his right mind would do. 'Stead of spending it uptown or carryin' it to Greenville, we held on to it. Lemme tell you, boy, money's like grease. It'll sho run right outta yor hand if you don't squeeze it tight. Savin' is squeezin', boy. If you ain't squeezing, you ain't savin'. That's what the folks uptown do you know—they figgers out how to make money work. Now me and Mae git a little mo' money ever' month from somebody else's pocket."

Uncle Cleve's school was in session, and as his only student, I continued to listen as his face lit up with pride over having the wherewithal to do what he knew had been good and profitable. Others laughed at him and called him a man who had no fun because he did not spend his money wildly and unwisely or in places to be seen and heard. On the other hand, he never had to knock on a door late at night to hurriedly borrow cash, as so many others had to do. No, he was following his own code of conduct.

For Uncle Cleve, having fun was having a future, not a moment. This meant that he often went without things others felt necessary for life. He didn't see the need to use his hard earned money to impress others who often had much less than him. He wore the same pair of brogan shoes year in and year out. It may have bothered others, but it didn't bother him. His clothes were washed and ironed over and over again. He didn't need new clothes simply because his business had done well. When others were trying to buy new and updated cars or trucks, he was fixing and repairing his own, getting just a few more miles out of it. There were many days I stood by his side and watched as he tinkered with his truck.

"Uncle Cleve, you gonna fix that oil leak yourself?"

"Why shorely I is, boy. You gotta learn to keep 'em up. Some folks cain't wait to go out and git a new truck, but not me. This truck is gonna outlast me, and if you ain't careful, it'll outlast you."

Needless to say, he never bought a new truck, and his old truck never let him down. This way of living allowed him to put money aside for future use. He became his own bank. In his day, he had very little choice. He warned me of having long eyes and no money of my own. I remember that conversation as well. It was just the two of us riding alone in the cab of his pick-up. He was looking straight ahead, but I could feel his eyes all over me as he talked.

Clifton Taulbert and Gary Schoeniger

"Cliff, if you got your own money, then you ain't beholden to nobody else. Mae and me can do things 'cause we got the money. When we want something, I don' have to borrow one thin dime from somebody's grocery store uptown and end up spending the rest of my life trying to pay it back or losin' everthang I own to do it. It's a sin and a cryin' shame, but folks do that, you know; every day they sink themselves in debt. I have my own money. Now where you think I got it?"

Before I could squeeze out an answer, Uncle Cleve answered his own question. "I saved it up, a little bit here and a little bit there. That's how you do it, boy, you save it up. Like I said, just 'course you got two dime, that don't mean you gotta spend 'em both. I ain't about to give them juke joints my hard earn money." At that point it was if he was talking to others who weren't there. He had his conversation while eyeing the multitude of bars and clubs we were passing. Although I was just a teenager, I was aware of the allure of Saturday nights in Glen Allan, but not of the financial consequences of those seductive evenings. Saturday nights were enticing to so many, young and old, but not Uncle Cleve. He made his money, and he held on to it. He was trying to catch me early in life, so that I could start off on the right foot.

Yes, Uncle Cleve made and kept his money and not under his mattress or in a trunk covered by quilts and secured with a double lock, but at the bank in Greenville, Mississippi. Uncle Cleve took money *to* the bank instead of *out* of it on a regular basis. That was so unusual to me. For a long time, I didn't know that you could take money to the bank. My folks lived from paycheck to paycheck. Early on, Ma Ponk kept her money under the mattress in the front bedroom. At that time in my life, before going to the bank with Uncle

Cleve, I figured the tall, stately, pillared building to be a place where only white people went. I could see people coming and going, but I don't recall any of them looking like me. I never dreamed that one day I'd go inside. Uncle Cleve changed all of that. Despite the fact that he could not enter through the front door, and had to go in through a colored entrance at the side, I was still in awe of just being with him and witnessing his grown-up banking transactions.

I was really taken with his passbook—his proof of his holdings. I saw him take his money and give it to the white person behind a cage and then slip his passbook to him. I'd watch the man write in his passbook and slide it back to him. Without much conversation passing between them, I watched as Uncle Cleve tucked his passbook into a secure pocket, cleared his throat, and smiled slightly as we walked out by the same side door we had entered. With his money safely tucked away, we headed back to Glen Allan where he would work just as hard as he had the week before and where he would expect just as much from me.

I still laugh when I think of what he told me that first day I went to the bank with him. "Boy, save fitty cents out of every dollar you makes and you ain't never gonna hafta borrow a dime from a soul." I was still a mere teenager in Glen Allan, Mississippi, living in a place where 20 cents would buy a loaf of bread, but somehow, Uncle Cleve was planting good seeds for my future harvest.

Clifton Taulbert and Gary Schoeniger

UNCLE CLEVE'S MESSAGE

Uncle Cleve was internally driven and he understood that his choices and actions rather than his circumstances would ultimately determine the outcome of his life. It was this fundamental shift in his perspective that separated him from others. It was a subtle yet profound transformation that empowered him to succeed.

He spent his time and energy only on things that would improve his life in the long term and lead him toward his goal. And his approach to money was no different.

Rather than spending his money to buy unnecessary things or to impress others, Uncle Cleve saw money as a tool to invest in his future, a tool that would enable him to create wealth. He was future-focused and willing to make sacrifices to get where he wanted to go. He was willing to live beneath his means because he valued financial freedom (his goal) more than he valued the opinions of others.

Temptations surrounded him just as they did others, yet he developed the ability to subordinate an impulse to a higher value—to his goals, his hopes, and his dreams. He did not drive expensive cars nor eat in fancy restaurants. He avoided the credit trap that so many others fell into. His shoes were old and his clothes were worn yet he took money to the bank, and his deposits always exceeded his expenses.

And while his money accumulated in the bank, his mind was focused on his next opportunity. Rather than being paid by the hour in a job where someone else controlled his future, Uncle Cleve was focused on solving problems and creating value for others and he understood that he could do that by focusing on saving his income. That way, when an opportunity presented itself, he had the resources to take action.

NO LONGER ENTERING THE BANK'S SIDE DOOR

Nearly all that I learned from Uncle Cleve traveled with me and does so even today. When I first moved to St. Louis and had a hard time finding a job, I recall that upon getting my first paycheck from Scrugg's, the department store where I washed pots and pans in their cafeteria, I took that $35 paycheck straight to the bank on Grand Avenue, which was right around the corner from where I was staying and opened up my very first savings account. I withdrew only $15 to live on and pay for necessary expenses such as rent and food. And just like Uncle Cleve, I treasured my passbook. Walking out of the bank, I felt as if I was on cloud nine. I only had $20 left, but I knew that it would grow. I would see to that.

Uncle Cleve also taught me about interest. It was difficult to stretch my meager earnings and to still save, but I did the best I could, and sent a few dollars back home every month to my mother. In addition, I was no longer in Glen Allan, but living in a city that was demanding more of me socially. My new friends dressed much better than I did. They went out for dinner, a new experience for me. But I couldn't see spending all my money on clothes and food. I wanted to dress well too, but somehow the lessons from Uncle Cleve permeated my thinking. After a while, my friends teasingly called me cheap, just like people back home did my uncle. I wasn't cheap, I was just being thoughtful. I had no one to fund my endeavors in life. I was on my own. I wanted to feel the same confidence Uncle Cleve did. I didn't want to be beholden to anyone. So week after week, I made my small deposits at the bank, and each time I did, I felt good.

Back home, I had never heard of a surplus clothing store. We just wore hand-me-downs that had been double-patched. But there was one in St. Louis. And so, in order to keep making deposits, I wore suits from a surplus clothing store that I had altered by Miss Missy, a lady who lived across the street. Of course I wanted better eventually, but it didn't bother me. My eyes were on my future. My confidence was coming not from what I wore, but from my own code of conduct. Ultimately, I was able to buy myself a brand new suit, one that was my size and not from a surplus store, but only after I felt I could do so without significantly altering my growing assets.

My response to the role of money in my life didn't change, even after I entered the United States Air Force. As soon as I got settled in my permanent duty, I opened up a bank account. Again, despite temptation all around me to spend money to fund a good time, I did otherwise. By now, I had no problem saving and ignoring those who accused me of being a cheapskate. I just knew that I had to have my own money and, as Uncle Cleve had said, if I spent what I earned, somebody else would have it and not me. This attitude stayed with me throughout my military career and on into Tulsa, Oklahoma, where I eventually ended up living, working, marrying, and starting my family. It was soon evident to anyone who knew me that I was no spendthrift. My younger brother, Claiborne, often would tease me by saying that I still had the first dollar I ever made. I was a saver, always anticipating that an opportunity could come along and change my life. From Uncle Cleve, I had learned to be ready and to parlay opportunity into action. Like him, I cultivated the continued expectation to see my circumstances change. If I needed to build a garage to work on high-dollar cars, I would need the money to buy a lot and build the building. I knew that my future, and the future of my family, depended upon my being prepared. After a while, I stopped looking for surplus stores hidden away off the main highway, but to this day I treasure bargains and sales. The greater the reduction, the happier I am.

More than anything, Uncle Cleve's life showed me that I could have a successful future, and that I didn't have to settle for a status quo that had been predetermined by someone else.

After the Air Force and once in Tulsa, my career took me from being a retirement community administrator to actually working inside the Bank of Oklahoma. This time I wasn't a messenger, and I didn't have to wear that humiliating messenger's uniform. I wore a suit with a white-collared shirt and tie. Even there, I took every advantage to save and solidify our financial growth as best I could, observing others and learning what I didn't know. And just like at Jefferson Bank and Trust years earlier, I embarked upon the bank graduate studies program, only this time, I had study partners and was not the only black person in my class—though I could still count the black participants on one hand. It was as if all the seeds that had been planted in the cab of Uncle Cleve's truck were breaking through the soil of my mind and sprouting at just the appropriate time in my life. More than anything, Uncle Cleve's life showed me that I could have a successful future, and that I didn't have to settle for a status quo that had been predetermined by someone else.

It's amazing how our mind holds on to things from our past. Perhaps it was precisely because banking was off limits to black professionals when I was growing up in the Mississippi Delta that I felt pulled in that direction. But the employment situation for black people in that world was no different in the city of St. Louis. Nonetheless, I felt drawn to somehow make banking a more concrete part of my life, not this mysterious place from which I either looked in

115

from the outside or only participated in as a customer. So in Tulsa, I looked for employment in the banking industry. It wasn't an easy pursuit, but I persisted. Finally, with help from Mr. Bill Welch, a white banker in Tulsa, I was hired into Bank of Oklahoma's management training program. With that job I felt as if I had fulfilled an emotional quest. Little did I know that the seeds planted on my first trip to the Greenville Bank with Uncle Cleve would yield a much greater harvest, one I would not have dared to dream of as a child growing up in Glen Allan, Mississippi, living in the shadow of thousands of rows of cotton fields that beckoned everyone else in the community.

Perhaps it was precisely because banking was off limits to black professionals when I was growing up in the Mississippi Delta that I felt pulled in that direction.

Flash forward. For several years, my wife, Barbara, and I were part of an investing group that started and sold one of the most successful de novo banks in Oklahoma's banking history. (A de novo bank is simply a newly chartered state bank that has been in operation less than five years.) It all started with a nighttime phone call from a friend, Tom Bennett, who called to tell me about his new business, this bank he was starting. We had met several years earlier and he had attended one of my seminars on the power of building community in the 21st century. Over the years, our relationship grew. So I was not surprised when he called to tell me about his latest venture, especially after he had retired from banking as a successful executive. I had thought back then that he was well on his way to becoming an important leader for our nation. He was just that type of man. However, during that call, my own entrepreneurial spirit kicked in, and I persisted in prodding him about this opportunity. I wasn't hearing everything I wanted to hear, so our conversation continued. I kept inserting myself into his business, asking him every question that came to mind. Within a few days, he called again and this time, Uncle Cleve was smiling. "Clifton, would you and Barbara consider becoming investors in the Oklahoma National Bank?"

I will never forget that phone call. I was actually not anticipating that request. "Let us think about it," was my reply. I was nervous. I was excited. I was scared. Not that I had never thought of owning a bank, I surely had—especially when I was standing out in the cold at the door of Jefferson Bank and Trust in St. Louis, holding it open so that the white customers could quickly get inside. I wanted to own that warmth too, but this offer was different. This was about dividends. This was about taking a risk. This was about having seed money. All my life I had been putting money aside. That's what Uncle Cleve told me to do. So we had the money. But I was also fearful. We could lose it. Then as I thought about it, I realized that we could also win. I didn't have to catch the field truck. And I didn't have to go to the general store and create a debt that would last all my life. This opportunity had been heading my way since the day I had walked into the Greenville Bank by the side entrance in 1958. Just as Uncle Cleve had followed his gut and bought the ice all those many years ago and won, I would do the same. Barbara and I agreed to invest. Even though we were among the least affluent and lesser percentage-wise of the investors, we had put away funds for just that moment.

It was scary, but for us the risk was worth it. Eight years later, when we sold the bank, the return was more than we expected or could have imagined at the time. I would have loved the opportunity to walk Uncle Cleve into the lobby of that bank and tell him that I was one of the owners. Maybe, just maybe, that slight grin of his would have broken out into a big smile all across his face.

Yes, it was all so long ago, when he talked to me, a kid, about future opportunities that would come my way, opportunities that would require money to participate. I had heard him. I understood that the future included me. Because of Uncle Cleve, saving and expecting became part of my life. I still follow his advice to this very day.

THE TIMELESS APPLICATION

Decrease your expenses while increasing your income. These are two fundamental aspects of creating wealth that have empowered entrepreneurs for generations. And, like the other lessons Uncle Cleve passed along, they do not require anything you do not already have. They are simple concepts that anyone can apply.

Entrepreneurs tend to focus their attention on the things that will advance their goals. They tend to view money as a resource to be used wisely, a resource that will enable them to achieve their goals.

Let's face it, we all want to earn more money, and we all like nice things. Yet, it's not the lack of money that prevents us from prospering. More often than not, it's our lack of understanding about money and how to use it as a tool.

It's been said that if we were to amass all of the world's wealth in one place and then redistribute that wealth evenly among the entire population, that wealth would find its way back into the hands of its original owners.

Why is that? Why do the rich seem to get richer while the rest of us seem to languish and struggle to get ahead and never seem to make ends meet?

The answers may lie in our understanding of what it takes to create wealth and how to use money as a tool.

Most of us have never had any formal training about how to build wealth, and most of what we know about money we learned at home from our parents or by observing others around us. And, if we were lucky enough to come from a wealthy home, we might be fortunate enough to learn about how that wealth was accumulated. Yet none of these advantages provide a guarantee if you don't have the right mindset. The vast majority of us are left to figure it out for ourselves, and we often buy into an attitude that blinds us to opportunity and prevents us from prospering.

Some spend their money on things that create the appearance of wealth. They buy big homes and fancy cars. They eat in expensive restaurants and take exotic vacations—often choking themselves with debt in the process. Without realizing it, in their attempt to emulate wealth, they create habits that prevent them from ever achieving it.

Some increase their expenses as their income increases. Every pay raise brings a bigger house, a newer boat, or a nicer car. Again, this is an easy trap to fall into, and many well-off people consider this an acceptable way of life. With their income dedicated to living expenses, they find themselves on a never-ending treadmill that leaves little room for investment in things that will actually generate wealth.

Some people become focused on reducing expenses, yet they never consider increasing their income. They scrimp and save, clipping coupons and searching for bargains wherever they

Clifton Taulbert and Gary Schoeniger

can find them. They manage to eke out a miserly existence saving for a rainy day, yet it never occurs to them to focus on things that may increase their income.

This is because most of us have been conditioned to think about work as an exchange of time for money. We've been conditioned to work for "someone else," and we've learned to think about income in terms of how much we get paid by the hour, the day, the week, the month or the project. We've learned to accept the fact that someone else will determine our wages, and that because there are a limited number of hours in a day, there is a limit to how much we can earn.

Entrepreneurs have a different approach. Rather than trading time for money, entrepreneurs tend to think in terms of creating value—that is to say, solving problems for other people. The more problems they can solve, the more they can earn. Their business becomes a system for generating solutions at the same time they create wealth. This system is limited only by their own imagination and a willingness to try.

This fundamental shift in perspective can be transformative. Rather than spending money on unnecessary things, entrepreneurs learn to use money as they do their time. Because they are future-focused they are therefore willing to make sacrifices to achieve their goals.

Rather than allowing others to determine their income, entrepreneurs look for ways to find new customers, add new products, and search for new ways to solve problems. They understand that the more people they can reach, the more problems they can solve, and the more money they can earn.

This is a simple and timeless lesson. It does not require anything you do not already have. It is a powerful lesson that can enable you to create wealth regardless of where you are right now.

Hopefully, by now you recognize a pattern and a shift has begun to occur in you. As we saw in the previous lessons, the ability to create wealth is something anyone can learn and anyone can apply. Like the previous lessons it also starts with a shift in our awareness followed by a change in our behavior.

CHAPTER 6

BRAND

"A brand for a company is like a reputation for a person."
—JEFF BEZOS, Founder of Amazon.com

"You gotta do what you tell folks you gonna do."
—UNCLE CLEVE

CLIFTON'S ICE HOUSE MEMORIES

At the Ice House, I had to show up for work on time. Uncle Cleve did not accept excuses, and in this he was as tough on himself as he was on me. Our first day of work together set those expectations. It was very early, and I was a nervous, skinny boy, sitting on the bench at the Ice House looking westward. I could still see the moon. It had not completely sailed west. Glen Allan had not fully awakened, but Uncle Cleve was wide awake. Very few sounds of life could be heard other than our conversation. It was still dark, but if I turned and looked eastward, way past where Miss Bea Brown lived, I could see the sun

123

trying to break through the night. But we were already up and ready for work. Soon the sound of that first field truck would break through the silence. Uncle Cleve was laying out what he expected of me—telling me how to talk to our customers and about being on time. My job was not guaranteed. I had several weeks to prove my worth. Between stopping to put more Prince Albert Tobacco in his pipe, Uncle Cleve made sure I understood what was required of me. He talked, and I just sat there and listened.

"We start work early 'roun' here. Gotta be here 'fore the customer gits here. They ain't got no time to wait 'roun' on us. So I need you here right 'long wid me. I told Sis Ponk when I wanted you here. So turn that bed loose. If you late, you ain't got no job. You hear me now, don't you?"

I heard him loud and clear. And over the months and years that I worked for him, I was never late—and neither was he. Our customers never had to worry about pulling up to be greeted by a padlocked Ice House. When the customer pulled up and got out of the car or yelled his ice order from the cab of his vehicle, he saw us standing on the dock ready to serve. That's just the way it was. No one had to yell for Uncle Cleve to come out and do business. He expected the same of me. We started work early every day, and by the time the sun rose in Glen Allan, we had already served more than ten field trucks. My neat jeans were soon wet and the cuffs covered with sawdust from the Ice House floor. Over time, Uncle Cleve's customers— especially those who drove the field workers' trucks—came to expect his availability and punctuality. No matter what, they knew they'd have their ice. Because field work started at six in the morning, they needed Uncle Cleve's doors to be opened as posted. Not only was his punctuality commonplace, so was his attention to his personal behavior in the workplace as well as in our community where we lived.

I can still remember us riding along in his 1947 International pickup truck, with me crowded in the cab along side of him, both of us now at the end of the day, smelling of stale water and sawdust. We were both tired, but he was not too tired to tip his hat to the ladies we passed along the way, or to give a nod to the men and women we passed. Though he was one of them and lived right in the middle of our neighborhood, those to whom he tipped his hat or simply nodded his head nearly always responded in a way that conveyed their respect for him. From the ladies, it was usually, "How do, Mr. Cleve?" And from the men, their responses were more along the lines of "Afternoon to you, Cleve."

I'm not sure I knew what to make of all that I witnessed. I just knew that Uncle Cleve seemed to be treated differently. Maybe it was because he treated everybody with the utmost respect. Maybe it was because everyone knew what to expect of him. Uncle Cleve carried himself with a steadiness that even his white customers admired. Instead of calling him Cleve, they called him "Mormon." Using his last name was as close a sign of a white person's respect as you could get in those days.

He also made buying ice a pleasant experience. From the cleanliness of the Ice House to his own personal appearance, Uncle Cleve operated from his own code of conduct. Though the work was hard and he was dirty by the end of the day, he always started out fresh and pressed. Dressed in his green khaki pants and shirt, Uncle Cleve set his own standards. Somehow, he factored in the consistency of his grooming and personal dress as part of the success he wanted. Uncle Cleve thought about what he wanted his customers to see and the message he wanted to present, and that was passed along to me. In the fields, no one cared how you looked. At the Ice House I knew that I couldn't come to work looking just any old way.

Clifton Taulbert and Gary Schoeniger

*From the cleanliness of the Ice House
to his own personal appearance,
Uncle Cleve operated from his own
code of conduct.*

Throughout Glen Allan and the surrounding cotton communities, Uncle Cleve was known as the man who kept his word. It was commonly said among his family and friends that "y'all kin set yore clock by Cleve's word." I know this to be a fact. Whether regarding work, or doing a good deed for a neighbor, Uncle Cleve never veered from keeping his word. Whether he was delivering ice uptown to Mr. Jake's General store in Glen Allan, or picking up Ma Ponk to take her to Hollandale to visit her sister, everyone knew that his word was gold. Of course, his driving below the legal speed limit was legendary, but his pattern was set. He left early and arrived on time. Everybody knew this.

Over the years he had made his own determination about who he wanted to be and how he wanted people to see him. He couldn't control their opinions of him, but he was in control of what they observed of him. Day in and day out, Uncle Cleve remained steady. He did this even under overwhelming circumstances where lesser men would have cratered. He always found the internal resolve to stay true to himself. This was borne out again the night he took me along with him to Jackson, Mississippi to a Big Top Circus.

When he told me about the circus, I could hardly wait to tell Ma Ponk. By the time I got home, I was wet with sweat and so excited that my words were running over themselves. Ma Ponk had to slow me down. "Now jis wait, boy, I ain't goin' nowhere. Big Top? Now whatchu talkin' 'bout?" Ma Ponk finally got me to settle down enough to explain that Uncle Cleve was taking me to Jackson. That was big, even for her. "I guess that's alright. Sho' hope you don't git in Brother Cleve's way."

The night before we left I could hardly sleep. As I lay on my small cot, I tried to imagine how this big city would look and how being at a real circus would feel. My imagination ran all over the place. That Friday workday was longer than any Friday I remember. I thought the noon rush at the Ice House would last forever. Finally it ended, and with everything cleaned and locked up, we headed home. By the time I got home, I was ready for my bath. Ma Ponk already had the number-three tub, the big round tin tub with a number three permanently stamped in the center, filled with boiling hot water. I lost no time in shedding my soiled work clothes took a quick bath, dried off, and dressed in my best clothes. Just like Ma Ponk and anyone else who would be riding with Uncle Cleve, I was outside waiting by our gate when he arrived.

Of course, Ma Ponk was waiting with me and they talked for a bit. I wanted them to stop so badly so we could be on our way to Jackson! But whining or any sign of impatience would not have been tolerated by either of them. So I bit my tongue. Finally, Uncle Cleve started up the engine, and Ma Ponk walked away. I climbed into the cab, pushing books and newspapers aside so that I could settle in. Uncle Cleve just looked at me and smiled slightly. I know he could see the excitement written all over my face. Like I said, he wasn't much for conversation, but that early evening, he filled my head with stories about all that I could expect.

"Boy, I saw my very first Big Top in Memphis. Now that's sho some city. People were ever-where. Popcorn was like gravel, all over the ground and smellin' mighty good. It was all the animals, some like I ain't never seen before. When I seen the elephants, I could hardly believe my own eyes. Cliff, them some mighty big ones. I seen the black and white ones that

127

looked like mules or hosses. Can't thank o' the names right now, but you'll see 'em, pretty thangs, too. Yessir, you gonna have the time o' yore life."

As he relived his own memories, I could tell that he could hardly wait too. When he wasn't talking, he was clenching his pipe, both of us surrounded by the smell of that savory tobacco. All I could do was settle back for the evening of my life. Because Uncle Cleve drove the speed limit, I was able to count every rock and tree between Glen Allan and Jackson until it got too dark to do so.

Finally, the landscape began to change. I saw fewer and fewer cotton fields. Buildings began to appear, and more and more vehicles showed up. I saw bright lights everywhere. I was in the city! My eyes could hardly contain all I was seeing. I couldn't wait to get to the circus. When we finally did, there were cars and people everywhere. In Glen Allan, parking was never an issue, but that night in Jackson it was. We drove around and around till Uncle Cleve finally found a place to park his truck. I remember being excited and pressed tightly by the crowd of people rushing forth. With Uncle Cleve leading me, we got our tickets and found a seat under the big top about midway down the bleachers. I can still see us. We were surrounded by people. We had good seats. Uncle Cleve wasn't talking, but I could tell that he was excited too. He bought me my own bag of hot, buttered popcorn—a bag that I didn't have to share with anyone else. I really felt grown up. I waited for the entertainment to start. I wanted to see the elephants. I was so excited, it never occurred to me to look around at the audience. As far as I was concerned, it was just the two of us out for the time of our lives.

And just as the lights came up and the drums began to thunder and the crowd began to roar throughout the big tent, this burly white guy in a white shirt, suspenders, and bow-tie rushed over to us. Looking Uncle Cleve directly in the face, he told us we had to leave. With no remorse or concern over the joy of a young boy, he said, "Friday night ain't the night for n-----s." Uncle Cleve, without saying a word or even looking at the man, grabbed my hand and with my popcorn dropping along the way, we eventually found our truck and drove slowly back to Glen Allan in silence. He never talked about that humiliating experience, but I never forgot it.

The next day was Saturday, the half-day of work, and as usual he was waiting for me. Neither one of us spoke of what had happened. We just kept working, cutting, and selling ice. In my own mind, I was struck by how Uncle Cleve had kept his cool in the face of that insult. He had his own attitude. Despite the humiliating situation, he knew who he was. He had worked all his life to define himself and was not about to let an example of unleashed ignorance set him off on an entirely different course of action. He was Cleve Mormon. He owned the Ice House.

He had his own attitude.
Despite the humiliating situation,
he knew who he was.

Clifton Taulbert and Gary Schoeniger

UNCLE CLEVE'S MESSAGE

Uncle Cleve understood that problems were opportunities. He knew that if he could solve problems for other people, he could also empower himself. He also understood the power of being reliable and that his reputation was an essential aspect of his ability to succeed. He also comprehended that it was an aspect of his life that he could control.

Central to Uncle Cleve's success as an entrepreneur was the simple fact that he was reliable. The people in Glen Allan Mississippi knew they could count on him. They trusted him to solve their problems. They knew his word was his bond. They knew he neither gave nor accepted excuses. They knew they could set their clocks to Uncle Cleve.

Uncle Cleve had no patents to protect his ideas. His word was his "intellectual property." Reliability was his brand. It was the promise he made to his customers. And the more people knew that they could count on Cleve, the more opportunities he found. They not only trusted him to deliver ice, they also bought wood and coal from him in the winter, and they allowed him to repair their high-dollar cars.

And it was his commitment to his word that gave him confidence. It put the lift in his stride and the twinkle in his eye. Uncle Cleve was inner directed, and his reputation was something he could control. Although it would have been easy for him to do otherwise, Uncle Cleve did not discriminate. He treated everyone fairly. Even when he faced a situation where humiliation seemed the only outcome, Uncle Cleve managed to maintain his dignity. He refused, taking the high road and refusing to lower himself to someone else's dismal standards. By doing what he said he would do, rain or shine, he watched his business grow.

AN INTERNAL CODE OF CONDUCT

I became what I saw. From that first early morning in June of 1958, I had the privilege of watching a man define himself for himself. I saw a man not afraid to step out and do what he felt needed to be done to ensure the success he had envisioned for himself. Uncle Cleve created the conversation he wanted people to hold about him. This was true in our small neighborhood and for the larger Glen Allan community as well.

We all knew that, with Uncle Cleve, being on time was the norm. We knew that working hard was the norm. We knew that being honest was the norm. We knew that adhering to the law was the norm. We knew that Uncle Cleve gave out one message: "You can count on me." He kept his word. In front of his face or behind his back, he created the only conversation one could honestly hold about him. Some 50 years later, I am still amazed at his ability to set his own code of conduct when it would have been so easy to do otherwise. He refused to follow what tradition or others demanded of him. It could not have been easy. He was human just like any of us. He knew that his lifestyle was the butt of jokes for some. "Well, with Cleve," they would say, "you ain't got to guess. The Man's the same everyday." He didn't care. He continued to go to the bank every week of his working life to make his deposits. He would not have used terms such as marketing or branding, but that was what he did with the consistency of his actions. He was establishing his own image. I know the word image probably never entered his vocabulary, either. But trust me, he had one. And it was the accumulation of all he did and said.

In his own way, Uncle Cleve instilled many of those values in me. It just happened. As a young boy, I'm sure I couldn't have been happy with everything he laid out—like being limited to just two free sodas, no matter how hot it got. I learned that rules weren't meant to be broken. Because he never wavered, I had to learn to step up to his expectations of me. I can honestly say that his examples and poignant conversations served me well and continue to do so.

Uncle Cleve's example of how to chart your own course in life was not lost on me. Several summers after working at the Ice House, I was hired by the Hilton Food Store to do work that historically had been set aside for young white boys. I knew that I could not change my skin color, but I also knew that my performance was within my control. Like Uncle Cleve, I could set a high level of expectations for myself and live up to them. I knew what was required to be successful in the workplace.

Uncle Cleve taught me not to waste time. He taught me how to get the job done. He taught me about adhering to a schedule. I learned to get up early and to work late. I saw him respect all people, and I learned to do the same—the field workers who looked like me as well as the white plantation owners. I sacked groceries for every single person with the same degree of respect. Uncle Cleve had demanded this of me. Up until the time I graduated from high school, I worked at the store, earning a solid reputation along the way—even from some of those who would have historically ignored me. At the store, where tempers were raised and race was always a factor, it could have all gone another way for me. Looking back, I am certain that night in Jackson at the circus and Uncle Cleve's measured response contributed to preparing me for my job at the general store. For any reason, all that I had built up could have easily been destroyed with just one outburst from me, no matter if it was justifiably provoked. Fortunately, Uncle Cleve had shown me a different path.

As a high school student working for him, I was shown how to establish my own internal code of conduct. I learned those lessons so well; I found it difficult to think and act otherwise. I wasn't used to having ready excuses. Having to travel nearly 100 miles round-trip every day, it would have been easy for me to drop out of school. I didn't. I just buckled down and studied hard. I knew how important learning was. From the Ice House to the grocery store, from the St. Louis bank to the Air Force, my actions continued to define who I wanted to become.

Somewhere along the way, I figured out that following the crowd was not what I wanted for my life. I outperformed what was expected of me. I washed pots and pans better than anyone else while also pounding the pavement to find something better. And when I did go to work at the bank, in spite of how I felt about being a uniformed doorman and messenger, no one was able to say I didn't do my job well. I didn't like it, but I did it well. This helped me later when I took it upon myself to attend banking school. No one could say that my work had not been noticed or give the bank reason not to finance my request. By then all of this forward thinking had become second nature for me. I had absorbed the lessons from Uncle Cleve and made them part of my life.

It was no different in the military. I excelled. My work ethic and my treatment of the people around me shaped how others viewed me. My reputation in basic training followed me to technical school in Amarillo where I ended up becoming a squadron leader. My peers and command superiors saw the consistency in the way I handled my life. Like Uncle Cleve, I dictated the conversation by what I did every day. When I finally received my permanent base assignment, my reputation had preceded me, and soon I ended up working in the commander's office. I guess you could say that I have been building my image for as long as I can remember. As you recall, the last years of my four-year commitment to the Air Force were spent in the 89th Presidential Wing in Washington, D.C. and that a top-secret security clearance had been necessary to determine the qualities of my reputation. Who is this airman?

What was he like in Glen Allan? How did he live his life in St. Louis? My friends, relatives, and employers had to talk about me, and I would not be present to coach their answers. My reputation spoke for me.

When I started my marketing business, years after the military, after completing college, graduate school, and working various jobs, there certainly were things I didn't know. I could have known more about accounting and finance. I was somewhat prepared. I certainly did not have all the financial strength I needed, but I had the internal currency needed to be successful in the long haul. Remember Stairmaster, one of my first really big opportunities? It was stressful, but I knew what would be required of me. Once I sold my first machine, I realized that I was an integral part of the sale. I knew that my clients would be buying me and my reputation, not just the machines that I was offering. Integrity and trust mattered. I recognized that the same "wind" of challenge that Uncle Cleve and so many others faced and continue to face would also blow in my face—and that I would be powerless to stop the wind. I knew I had to focus on those things within my control—my reputation and integrity being two of them. I knew that my word was good. I could be trusted. I knew how to treat people. I knew what to demand of myself. I knew how to set myself apart from the herd.

I certainly did not have all the financial strength I needed, but I had the internal currency needed to be successful in the long haul.

THE TIMELESS APPLICATION

As an entrepreneur, your brand is your reputation. It is the promise you make to your customers. It is the message you send to the world about who you are and what you stand for. Rather than a clever slogan or a fancy logo, your brand is the result of your actions, and your actions stem from your beliefs.

After all, entrepreneurs are problem solvers. They see problems as opportunities and they understand that by solving problems for other people, they can also empower themselves. Therefore, as an entrepreneur, we must develop a reputation for being reliable—as someone who can be trusted—if we are to succeed.

Being reliable—doing what you say you're going to do, when you say you're going to do it, for the price you agreed to do it—is a critical aspect of being a successful entrepreneur. Being reliable will build your brand and expose you to more opportunities. The more people know they can rely on you, the more problems they will count on you to solve and the more your business will grow.

Being reliable can also become a competitive advantage that will enable you to stand out. It can also present opportunities that others overlook.

This is a simple concept, one that has empowered entrepreneurs from sole proprietors and small-business owners to some of the greatest success stories of all times.

Ted Moore and his daughter Sirena created a multimillion dollar cleaning company by providing a simple yet reliable service that their customers could count on. Starting from scratch, Lydia Gutierez grew Hacienda foods to 85 employees by offering a valuable product and building a reputation for being reliable. Howard Schultz transformed Starbucks from a

135

coffee shop into an empire by providing friendly and reliable service for an otherwise mundane experience. Reliability is a basic concept that can expose a world of unlimited opportunities, regardless of where you are right now.

As an entrepreneur, we must learn to look at the world through the eyes of our customers and ask ourselves a few simple questions:

- Why should someone buy my product or service?
- How will they know I will do what I say?
- Why should they believe in me?
- What are others saying about my product or service?

Your brand is your reputation, the promise you make to your customers and the message you send out to the world. As an entrepreneur, you must be able to convey to your customers that you can be relied upon to solve their problems, that: "You can count on me."

Your brand is more than a logo, a website, an ad, or a sign. It is not what you say that is important. Your brand is the reputation you acquire as the result of what you do. Actions speak so loudly they drown out words. Your behavior must be consistent with your words. As Uncle Cleve demonstrated, this is an aspect of your life over which you clearly have control.

Your brand is a message that must convey confidence and reliability. It is also a message that can be communicated in a variety of ways—many of which are subtle and unspoken but are often more powerful than anything you can say.

Being on time conveys confidence and reliability—and showing up early sends a clear message that you are someone who is eager to solve problems and get the job done. Neatness and proper attire are important aspects of your brand. Good posture, direct eye contact, and a firm handshake all convey confidence and contribute to the message that you are someone who will do what is promised.

Consistency conveys confidence. Like Scotch tape, your solution must work every time. No excuses. If people know they can count on you, they will tell others, and your world will begin to expand. Going above and beyond, doing more than is expected of you is a way to build a reputation as someone who can be counted on.

Entrepreneurs understand that their success reflects on their ability to solve problems for others. Rather than making excuses or promises they cannot keep, entrepreneurs are service-oriented. They take initiative and tend to do more than is expected of them rather than less. And, by doing so, the word gets out and their world continues to expand.

Being consistent and reliable also builds confidence. The more reliable you become, the more your confidence in what you do will grow. And, the more confident you become, the higher you will reach and the more opportunities you will encounter.

Reliability is a simple concept that anyone can apply. It does not require a patented new technology, intellectual property, or an MBA. It is the great equalizer, like a lever that enables you to move up in the world. It is a simple skill that can empower anyone to overcome obstacles and improve their own lives.

As an entrepreneur, your words must match your actions, and your reputation becomes your brand. The more people that know you can be counted on to solve problems, the more opportunity you will encounter and the more your world will continue to expand. As an entrepreneur, reliability will become a way of life. More than a clever slogan or a fancy logo will, being reliable soon becomes a habit, one that conveys authority and security and becomes part of who we truly are.

Establishing your brand, defining your reputation, and being reliable not only defines the successful entrepreneur, but also provides a shift in thinking for anyone who is determined to maximize their potential and reach for a better life.

Clifton Taulbert and Gary Schoeniger

This is the power of the entrepreneurial mindset: its avail-ability to any one of us, regardless of our circumstances or our age. The entrepreneurial mindset is not limited to just those seeking to build a business. It can empower anyone in work and in life. Whether we are in business, in school, or transforming our lives, it is essential to understand that wherever we are, in whatever we do, we are all building our brand.

CHAPTER 7

COMMUNITY

"Tell me the company you keep and I'll tell you who you are."
—MIGUEL DE CERVANTES, DON QUIXOTE

"You need friends, all us do, but picking good ones is up to you."
—UNCLE CLEVE

CLIFTON'S ICE HOUSE MEMORIES

From my very first day at work, excited and scared, to my very last day, confident and assured, I heard Uncle Cleve's opinions about choosing the right friends.

"Boy, even God's birds know how to fly with birds goin' the same place. You just gotta choose yoreself some good friends. That's how we git in trouble, listenin' to people who jest about lost already. Strike up with folks in school. Ain't nothing to that little fun at them juke joints. Hangin' out wid all of 'em there can lead to trouble. Take my word, boy, I's young once myself."

Clifton Taulbert and Gary Schoeniger

He was very adamant about it, too. And even though, at the time, I didn't understand all that he was saying, I had learned to respect him and to value his words. Most times, we'd be just sitting around on the Ice House porch waiting for customers or crowded into the cab of his pickup truck when he would caution me about how the wrong crowd could change the direction of my life without my control. He would also point out to me young people and adults who had made good choices and how good their lives were looking. Even though I was barely into my teenage years, looking back, I realize that he was catching me at my most vulnerable time. Over the years, we had many talks, but one in particular stays with me. I can still hear his words and feel the stifling heat as we sat crowded in the cab of his truck.

We were driving from the Ice House that day toward uptown where we'd come to a fork in the road. By taking the left fork, we were on the partially blacktopped road that led to the neighborhood where we all lived. By going this way, we would pass by several juke joints, including Mr. James Gatson's café, the place where noted Blues singers came to perform, and quite a few other bars—all venues that were extremely alluring, but off-limits to me. I could never go there, but I loved imagining what it was like inside.

My friends, however, in spite of our ages being the same, saw the insides of the juke joints on a regular basis. I remember their detailed conversations in the schoolyard about the fun goings on inside. But from Ma Ponk and others, I also heard about the trouble that seemed to always take place as well. It all sounded so exciting! I was at an age where children want to disobey their parents and other authority figures. Uncle Cleve knew this, and whenever he could, he took the opportunity to lay the foundation for me to make good decisions. I know this now, but at the time, I just listened, not fully aware of just how important his conversations would be in my life. And so it began on that hot Glen Allan day several generations ago.

He seemed to have been filled with wisdom. I don't know where it all came from, but he had a wellspring somewhere inside of him that always seemed to run freely when we were alone on the Ice House porch or in the cab of the truck. This day would be no different as we passed juke joint row, as I now call it. He took every opportunity afforded him to point out the trouble those places offered. He was right. As we drove slowly by them with the intoxicating sounds of the blues seeping into the cab of his truck, he looked straight ahead. He was one to always keep his eyes on the road. Just like him, I looked straight ahead while drinking an RC Cola, my last free one. Then he cleared his throat and started to talk. "Boy, everbody ain't got your best interests at heart." That's all he said for awhile. The words just hung in midair. I guess he had to let it sink into my teenage head before he went further. While he was waiting for his words to sink in, I felt the truck slowing down a bit, which was somewhat difficult to do considering how slowly he drove. Out of the corner of my eye, I watched as he turned and stared out of his side window. I saw a couple of my young school friends hanging around a juke joint. Somehow, I knew that they were going to get woven into his conversation, even though I acted as if I had not seen them. I was right.

Uncle Cleve cleared his throat again. "Look at 'em. See them boys over there?" I saw them standing in the alleyway between Mr. Gatson's juke joint and another house that had recently been converted to a bar. I knew those kids. We had all grown up together, but they had a lot more freedom than I did. I wasn't permitted to just hang out with the guys (even if I had had the time to), and I had a curfew that was absolute. They had already learned to smoke and could roll dice with the best of the grownups. They were hip—"had it all-together" as we called it back then—but not so to Uncle Cleve. He was advising me from a place I was too young to see or understand.

141

"Boy, I kin tell you, they kin git in a heap o' trouble. Ain't too much good comin' out of a place like dat. I know y'all know one 'nother, but be careful. Mind my word, boy, you'd best be careful."

"Yessir," I answered, not sure of what was next, but fully aware that the conversation was not over. He nodded and started up again.

"Better be like Ponk's boy Sidney and git something in yore head. I'd a git wid the ones goin' somewheres—you know, them that ain't scairt to pick up a book. Ain't nothing to field work. Git sumpin' in yore own head."

By now we had passed the juke joints and were almost to Miss Florence's store. I enjoyed delivering ice to her small store. She'd always give me a Jack's cookie—a delicious treat soaked in butter and cinnamon and soft to the bite. However, as we rounded the bend in the road, we dodged a couple of people who were walking around, clearly inebriated, and paying no attention. That spurred Uncle Cleve to pick up his conversation. "Yeah, them places kin be fun. I wuz young once, but lemme tell you, some of them people in them places can pull you right down to the ground. Trus' me, I know. You gittin' up there in age and gonna have girls on yore mind, so be careful. You gotta take care of the family name. You ain't got much if you mess up and lose your name. "

The second time he mentioned family name, he turned and looked at me. I guess he wanted to make sure that I had grasped how important it is to choose relationships wisely. I am not sure I fully understood everything he was telling me, but I took it to heart. Maybe it was the way in which he talked and the fact that it was just the two of us squeezed in together in the cab of his truck. I felt sort of grown-up, as if I was hearing something that I might not otherwise. He had his pipe, and I had my bottle of RC Cola.

He kept talking, and I kept listening. "Cliff, you gonna need friends, all us do, but you gotta pick 'em right."

I didn't quit talking with my childhood friends. We all went to school together and lived within the same neighborhood. Our neighborhood was too small to just cut them off. I simply made sure that their jive-talking conversations did not influence my actions. I knew instinctively when to leave their company—even if I wanted to stay. Way back then, Uncle Cleve's conversations had already begun to define my life. We never deconstructed in detail the reasons to be careful of these particular friends. They were, for all practical purposes already adults in our small farming community. It wasn't all their fault; Uncle Cleve's world was just so different. After school and work, they seemed to be in control of their leisure time—some of which would be spent in places that I wanted to go, but was forbidden to do so.

Lazy can slip in on you 'fore you know it. And lazy sho don't like to leave.

I was able to make good decisions not because I was so wise, but because Uncle Cleve kept talking day after day, picking up where he had left off. The man never let up. I can still hear him. "If they keep up what they doin', I kin tell you, they ain't gonna 'mount to much. They need ta be workin'. Lazy can slip in on you 'fore you know it. And lazy sho don't like to leave." Maybe he knew how easy it would be for me to fall in with the other boys. Yet, while he wanted more for me, I would later learn that I had to want more for myself. Wanting more would dictate with whom I chose to surround myself.

143

That day, however, we finally made it to the back of Glen Allan where we all lived. Because Uncle Cleve drove so slowly, it took a while to weave our way through. Ma Ponk was standing in the doorway looking out behind her screen door. When she knew it was us, she stepped out and waved. Uncle Cleve tipped his hat as I jumped out of the truck with my warm bottle of RC Cola.

UNCLE CLEVE'S MESSAGE

Because he was future focused, Uncle Cleve taught himself to stick with others who were the same. He made the choice to create the life he wanted rather than the life everyone around him had accepted.

Uncle Cleve chose to focus his time and attention on things he could change, on the aspects of his life over which he had control. He had little time for the juke joints and neighborhood saloons. He did not engage in gossip and small talk. Instead he earned the respect of others and created a community of respect, a network of action-oriented individuals who shared his commitment to success. He earned the respect of others, and he paid attention to what other business owners were doing.

Uncle Cleve was a student as well as a teacher. He learned from the success of others and, thankfully, he was willing to pass along what he had learned.

A DARK CLOUD HANGING OVER MY HEAD

Today I know just how important those conversations were about choosing the right friends and being able to look beyond the moment to the future. I have no doubt that choosing the right relationships along the way has made a critical difference in my life. I doubt that Uncle Cleve could even imagine the work I do and the people I encounter from all over the world. I know when I worked for him I had no idea that I would one day lecture at Harvard University and the University of Chicago. I had heard of neither while growing up. In fact, I didn't even know about all the historical black colleges. I never looked beyond the fields of the delta which had defined our outlook for all times. All I wanted to do was stay out of the fields and to make something of my life, but I was unsure of how that something could look. In the midst of that reality was Uncle Cleve, clearing his throat, smoking his pipe, and pointing out a path for me to take. He didn't know where it would lead, but he did know that if I took the wrong path, I would never experience the future as it could be. It has worked out for me, but I am smart enough to know that it all could have been different had I not chosen to listen to those timeless lessons from that ordinary man. I had many opportunities to choose the wrong path—to choose the wrong friends— but opted otherwise.

I have continued to follow his advice—advice that allowed him to set himself apart in a world where tradition had already decided the outcome for his life. In that small world he determined his own journey and realized along the way that he had the responsibility to chose the friends he wanted to travel with him and to not choose others who would have undermined his plans.

*I had no idea that I would one day
lecture at Harvard University.*

There must have been a time in his young life when
Uncle Cleve discovered that he had to make a decision about
the company he kept. I'll never know what that moment
was. I just know that he consistently made me aware of
what I should do and the consequences of my behavior
should I stray.

And nowhere was this more important than when I was
a young airman in the United States Air Force. Of all of the
times I had to make significant relationship decisions, this was
indeed a deciding moment my life. I was still young with my
future in front of me. I was still impressionable. I was at that
place in my life when others' opinions mattered. I wanted to
be part of the group. I was a normal young man like all the
others around me. Had I chosen unwisely in that world, and it
was so easy to do, I feel that my future would have followed an
entirely different path.

While in St, Louis, shortly after graduating from high
school in Mississippi, I was fortunate in my choice of friends,
many of whom are still my close friends today. But the Air Force
was different. I was not yet 20 years old but by the time I was in
the Air Force, my volition was already leading me in the right
direction. I tried always to keep in mind that something better
existed. Uncle Cleve had started that process years earlier. My
disappointment with my jobs in St. Louis had motivated me
to reach for better, rather than accepting less of myself. I had
somehow grasped the understanding that my own efforts could
alter the course of my life. I was beginning to understand what
was possible. However, the military would exist as an entirely
different proving ground.

It was in the mid 1960s and, as I have said, being shipped off to Vietnam was more the rule than the exception for young soldiers. Knowing this and with our basic training completed, many of my young friends used this as the excuse to throw caution to the wind and to have as much fun as possible within the time they felt they had left. It was also the age of Motown and the intoxicating voices of Aretha Franklin and Diana Ross as well as the era of the flower children. Recreational drugs, mostly underground back then, were slowly entering our daily lives. The Civil Rights movement had come of age and young people were mingling with people they had once been segregated from. The world was changing around me, and with all of that, it looked as if Vietnam was in my future.

My permanent assignment after basic training at Dow Air Force Base in Bangor, Maine, would be a test. Basic training was highly supervised and regulated; thus I did not have to think very much about relationships and what my choices could mean for my future. I would learn that being permanently assigned would provide a greater degree of personal freedom and choice, since I was away from home and away from those voices that could keep me going in a positive direction. Now I was on my own. It was a time when I'd need every lesson that Uncle Cleve had planted in my fertile young mind. I might be a thousand miles away from the juke joints of Glen Allan, but those childhood buddies from Glen Allan still surrounded me. They had different names and different hometowns now, but they were just as persuasive. With the weight of war hanging over our heads, it was so easy to embrace the present, especially when you felt the future might never come. It was a time and place where questionable activities and "good times" could be easily organized. Once basic training was over and real military life

Clifton Taulbert and Gary Schoeniger

began, whether we were stationed at home or abroad, these possibilities would force me to think about the company I wanted to keep. The decisions I made while in the military could impact me for the rest of my life.

I had my internal barometer of what was right and wrong, but the voices around me were loud and persuasive.

But by the time I arrived at Dow Air Force Base, a social culture had already been established, and it revolved primarily around recreation and pleasure—having a good time all the time. A soldier's social life featured many of the activities that Uncle Cleve had lectured me to shun. I had my internal barometer of what was right and wrong, but the voices around me were loud and persuasive. It was difficult not to hear them. I wanted the good times. I wanted to be part of the crowd. I didn't want to be left out. When the opportunities to party came my way, I wanted to join in yet somehow I hesitated. I noticed that many of my fellow soldiers talked only about the night before. They rarely mentioned the future or what their lives might look like beyond the military. I could feel myself being slowly drawn into their thinking, even though I knew better. Their voices were loud and inviting. I knew I had to make choices. Making the right choices hadn't been easy while growing up in Glen Allan—but Uncle Cleve and others were there to help focus my thinking. Not so here. I was on my own. I was no longer working at the Ice House. Uncle Cleve was no longer looking me in the face and telling me to protect the family name. I had to step up. But could I?

"Professor, who you think you is?" my military friends said to me.

"You a soldier just like us. You might as well act like us."

"We all goin' to the Silver Dollar saloon tonight, and you goin' with us!"

"You may as well enjoy your life; you goin' to Vietnam anyway."

Finally, the pressure became too great to just keep saying no. I caved in and followed the guys for a night out in Bangor that included the infamous bar under the bridge. I was clearly out of my element. There were women everywhere. Alcohol was being poured like it came from a water fountain. The smell of marijuana permeated the air. Everyone was dancing, making out, hitting on someone, getting drunk. Did I want this? I hesitated again. In that second I realized that I did not fit in. It took all the courage I had to walk away from the liquor, the drugs, the women, but I knew I had to find new friends.

Maybe back home in Glen Allan, my young friends also saw their lives as fruitless. After all, southern tradition had dictated our activities for generations. Maybe that's why they, like my military friends, decided to make the best of their lives as they saw it and invited me to come along. It would have been easy to do so. Fortunately for me, I worked for a man who viewed life differently. He saw himself in the future and sought to bring that same attitude into my life—a way of thinking that I needed as a young soldier on his own.

The friends I needed were there, but not in the places I had chosen to look early on. I had to move away from the rooms designated as our casinos where the seductive conversations about social plans continued nonstop. It took courage to set my own path, to remain friendly and not captive to the ideas of others. I had to get out of their company.

149

I started going to the library. Then I decided to enroll in college on campus at the University of Maine and added correspondence courses from the University of Maryland. It was in those places that I found a new set of friends—ones who were going my way. We strengthened each other's resolve and soon the jeering about not my having fun didn't matter. I had found my community. It was in this community of friends that I was encouraged to write—a profession that I had never ever considered. We were in the military, and we all had Vietnam hanging over our heads like a dark cloud, but as you know, I was fortunate. I was selected for a special assignment in Washington, D.C. at the 89th Presidential Wing. I can only say that choosing the right friends along the way made a significant difference in how my life turned out. I chose unselfish friends. They wanted me to succeed, and I wanted the same for them. We supported each other in making good decisions. We weren't perfect, but we embraced our core—for me, a core that had the handprints of life at the Ice House all over it.

Uncle Cleve had been right again. Choosing whom to hang with was my choice. It had been my choice when I was thirteen. It had been my choice when I attended high school in Greenville, Mississippi. It had been my choice when I had arrived in St. Louis. And it was again my choice when I became a soldier. Uncle Cleve had left me with some powerful lessons on how and why to choose as I had. I was in control again of my own future.

When my enlistment was up, I went back to college and was able to focus because of the entrepreneurial mindset that was driving me to succeed. I knew to surround myself with a community of people who were also headed in the "right" direction. When I started my first business fifteen years ago, I was selective in the friends I chose to travel alongside of

150

me. I wanted relationships with people who shared my values and whose values I mirrored. In so many words, this is what Uncle Cleve taught me. I still follow his lesson today. "It's up to you, boy." This lesson on creating your own community is as important to creating and sustaining the entrepreneurial mindset as all the other lessons discussed thus far—including the remaining mindset lesson: persistence.

THE TIMELESS APPLICATION

Entrepreneurs understand that life is not a lottery. They understand that their choices rather than their circumstances will ultimately determine the outcome of their lives.

They understand that their ability to choose the way they respond to their circumstances is perhaps the single most powerful ability we have as human beings. They comprehend the power of knowledge combined with effort, and they set out to seek the knowledge they need that will enable them to reach their goals.

They also understand the power of social influence and their ability to create an intentional community, a community of positive influence, knowledge, accountability, encouragement, and support. They get the importance of mentoring and guidance on their journey toward success.

As an entrepreneur, it is essential that we surround ourselves with successful models; that we create an intentional community of others who are also inner-directed, who are reaching for their goals and are willing to share their knowledge and experience and to reach out to and provide a hand.

While this idea of creating your own community of support may seem simple, it may not be easy. This is because old habits die hard, and cultural and environmental influences may discourage us from challenging the status quo, from leaving the life we have accepted in pursuit of the life we have imagined.

A closer look may provide some important clues.

In the past, entrepreneurs were often looked upon as mavericks that bucked the system. It was so much easier to look for lifetime employment that offered decent wages with a pension and benefits. Entrepreneurs were a small inscrutable bunch.

Today, entrepreneurs have become mainstream players who are driving our economy. Yet much about them remains shrouded in mystery and obscured by popular myths, while their habits and culture are not yet widely embraced.

Often, the social influences in our classrooms and communities can discourage us from thinking and acting differently, from being innovative and entrepreneurial and leaving the confines of the comfortable and familiar to challenge the status quo.

Social influence—also known as peer pressure—occurs when our thoughts, feelings, or actions are affected by other people. This subtle yet powerful influence takes many forms and can be seen in a variety of ways, none perhaps more pervasive than with the company we keep.

More often than not, we tend to identify and surround ourselves with people who think and act more or less like we do—those with similar interests and habits, ideas and ambitions. Without realizing it, we often surround ourselves with those who mirror our beliefs and have a similar mindset.

Without being aware of it, we often internalize the beliefs and assumptions of those around us. Unwittingly, we succumb to peer pressure, adopting the mindset of those around us and surrender our power to choose. Without realizing it, we relinquish our power and our responsibility for the outcome of our lives.

Some fail to understand the power of knowledge combined with effort and the willingness to try. Others are constrained by social influence and peer pressure rather than conscious choice.

Many of us do not understand what it is about entrepreneurs that allow them to succeed. Some may attribute their success to luck or privilege, things that cannot be controlled. Some regard entrepreneurs as wealthy larger-than-life figures—supermen whose success seems so unattainable, enormous, or complex that it often seems out of our reach.

Others may think of the superstars of the Silicon Valley —technology geeks who earn tens or hundreds of millions from companies they started in their garages or college dorms.

Some may equate entrepreneurs with greedy or unscrupulous behavior; the corrupt CEOs and Wall Street power brokers who sometimes make headlines.

And, because we tend to surround ourselves with like-minded people who think and act more or less like we do, many of us do not personally know any entrepreneurs. Nor do we take the time or the effort to read about them, to research their stories, and to learn the details about what they did and how they were able to succeed.

Experienced entrepreneurs have valuable knowledge and insight gained from their experience. The most effective ways to gain this knowledge is by asking lots of questions through regular interactions and from as many face-to-face meetings as possible. In other words, the most effective way to learn about entrepreneurship is through mentoring—gaining firsthand experience through other successful entrepreneurs.

More often than not, successful entrepreneurs are willing to share their experience and insight with others who demonstrate a willingness to learn. All we need to do is ask. Yet, if our image of an entrepreneur is outdated, if our only exposure to entrepreneurs are the larger-than-life or corrupt figures we see in the media, if we don't know any entrepreneurs and haven't taken the time to educate ourselves about the underlying beliefs and assumptions that drive their behavior, it's easy to make false assumptions—unchallenged assumptions—about what it was that enabled them to succeed.

Clifton Taulbert and Gary Schoeniger

Mentors play a vital role in nearly every entrepreneurial success story. They provide valuable knowledge and insight that can guide us through the challenges and uncertainties that we all must face. They become part of an intentional community—one that can introduce you to others who may be able to provide knowledge, resources and opportunities. Mentors can help you identify your strengths as well as your weaknesses. They can encourage you to keep going when you feel like giving up. They can also share in the joys of your success.

CHAPTER 8

PERSISTENCE

"Nothing in the world can take the place of persistence. Talent will not... Genius will not... Education will not... Persistence and determination alone are omnipotent."
—CALVIN COOLIDGE,
35th President of the United States of America

"As long as I kin wake up, I'm gonna git up."
—UNCLE CLEVE

CLIFTON'S ICE HOUSE MEMORIES

Being persistent is closely related to not being afraid to work hard. At the Ice House, persistence was not one of the words used to describe what was expected of you. I was an adult before that word became part of my vocabulary. Back home in Glen Allan, their way of expressing persistence was simply: work hard and don't give up. At the Ice House, this was communicated to me in words and in deeds as I watched Uncle Cleve build his business. The connection between persistence and hard work was understood from my very first day. By the way he worked and carried himself, it appeared that Uncle Cleve was well aware that giving up was not an option for him. I would later learn that giving up would not be one for me, either. He worked with a passion that others did not understand. In spite of the restricted social and economic climate that surrounded him, he was driven to succeed.

As a 13-year-old boy, I had no way of understanding the challenges that Uncle Cleve must have faced in establishing his business in that strictly segregated world. I find it difficult to believe, though, that he didn't face all sorts of challenges—challenges that could have lead him to throw in the towel. It was clear to me that whatever tests he had faced, he had also found a way to pass them. He knew what was possible. It's important to know that before the success at the Ice House, Uncle Cleve had also failed in business—a failure that didn't curb his appetite for independence. He was determined. I was very young, probably around six or seven, but I remember Uncle Cleve and Ma Mae when they were cotton farmers. I don't know how many years they worked this cotton dream before failure sent them in another business direction.

"Wake up, boy. Wake up!" I remember Mama Ponk's voice penetrating the covers on my small cot and after several turns. "Go on now, git ready. Elder Young gonna be here any minute. Put on that long sleeve plaid shirt. I know you gonna be in that cotton house. Bugs all over dat place. Come on now, you can eat at Mae's when we git there."

It was early fall in the delta and the fields were ripe with cotton. Nearly everybody in Glen Allan caught the field trucks and picked cotton for the big plantation owners, except for the few of us who held out some time to help the small independent colored farmers, who included Uncle Cleve. Over the years, Ma Ponk and several members of our family would help bring in his crop. Uncle Cleve and Ma Mae were both hard workers and even though the odds for success were against them, we all wanted to help them succeed. Although I was too young to be of any real use, I tagged along. Our workdays were routine, one day the same as the next. To recall one day is to recall them all.

I had a small sack to use for my "pickins," but nothing much was really expected of me. I was just being slowly brought into the system.

After Ma Ponk's wake-up call, I rushed to get dressed. Finally ready, I waited by the front gate for Poppa's car to pick us up. Everyone else called him Elder Young, but to me he was simply, Poppa, my great-grandfather who had one of the few cars in our neighborhood. Still somewhat sleepy, I would be stuffed in the back seat of the car between several adult aunts. No one was talking much. We were all still sleepy. For the adults, it was another day of work, but for me it was an adventure. I had a small sack to use for my "pickins," but nothing much was really expected of me. I was just being slowly brought into the system. I didn't care that it was early and the moon and the sun were still vying for space in the sky. I was in a car, and it was moving. Not only that, but I could hardly wait for the food Ma Mae had kept warm just for me. I also looked forward to seeing my big cousins, Joe and O'Neal, Uncle Cleve's teenage son and Ma Mae's teenage grandson. The boys lived with them and worked on the small farm. They always welcomed me to their world of work, and when I was not picking cotton into my small sack, my cousins would play with me, tossing me onto the piles of cotton stored in the cotton house or take me for rides on the back of the Ferguson tractor. I was too young to understand the challenge of growing and harvesting cotton. I was too young to know that they could fail.

At the end of the day, sitting on sacks of picked cotton, I'd watch as their output—the amount of cotton picked by each person— was tallied and as Uncle Cleve paid each picker in cash. It never occurred to me that it would end. But it did. Their farming business failed. One day Poppa no longer came to pick us up. I no longer had Ma Mae's delicious food waiting for me. I was no longer the human pillow my cousins tossed about. We no longer went out to Cleve's place. The memory of that time for some of us would fade, but I doubt that it was forgotten by Uncle Cleve. When failure does not tear you apart, it serves to spur you on. Somehow, I feel that the farm failure ignited my uncle's passion for his next endeavor: his success at the Ice House.

Even though I was young, I remember the sad and hushed conversations, bits and pieces from the older people who quietly informed each other that Cleve and Mae had to give up the farm. They weren't able to make a go of it. "Cleve and Mae had to give it up. I wonder what Cleve gonna do? They lost big."

And then they began to speculate what their next move might be. "I guess they can pick up some work 'roun' here somewheres. Mae's a mighty good cook. Anybody'll hire her. Cleve can work on thangs. He's good wid his hands, you know." Yes, all of that was true, but fortunately for me, Uncle Cleve had a different picture of his future. Failure did not stop him in his tracks.

I wish I could tell you step-by-step what happened after they quit farming. I have no memory of Uncle Cleve becoming a day laborer, although having failed could have sent him back to that established tradition. I do know that shortly after they moved all their stuff from the farm to Glen Allan and set up house, Uncle Cleve was back in business for himself, buying and selling ice throughout our community and surrounding areas.

Uncle Cleve never once told me to work hard. I knew from what I saw, and I knew what was expected of me. "Clifton, get a move on, you. We got to git dis here truck loaded. I hear the service station down by the lake is starting to sell ice. That's a'right. It's a free country you know." The "ice man," as he was affectionately called by some, lived with the same social constructs that sought to define all our lives in the pre-integrated south, but he possessed a mindset that kept his spirit free. Work to him was exciting, and working hard for himself was liberating. I feel certain that the daily process he engaged in lifted his sights beyond the barriers that sought to block him. I know it was hard, but he kept focused. Even while his modest monopoly would slowly slip away as technological change and competition found its way into our hometown, he continued to buy and sell ice with the same passion as if it was his first day.

UNCLE CLEVE'S MESSAGE

Life was not easy for Uncle Cleve. He worked hard every day. Yet, of all the "secrets" to his success, none is perhaps more powerful than persistence—his refusal to give up. And, like most entrepreneurs, his road to success was not without pitfalls, setbacks, and failures. Yet he knew that he could not fail as long as he refused to quit.

While many attribute success to an innate ability, luck, or circumstance, most overlook persistence, a subtle yet powerful mindset that Uncle Cleve surely understood.

Clifton Taulbert and Gary Schoeniger

It is persistence that will enable you to face challenges and overcome obstacles. It is persistence that will empower you to forge ahead in the face of fear and uncertainty and will encourage you to push yourself to find solutions.

Like our previous mindset lessons, perseverance is something we can all learn. It does not require specialized knowledge. It does not require a rare ability, an innate talent, or a genius IQ. It does not require access to money power or privilege. Perseverance and determination are traits we are all capable of. And, more often than not, perseverance is the key to creating success.

BEYOND MY WILDEST DREAMS

Uncle Cleve's example of being persistent and never giving up followed me and continues to do so. Hopefully, I have passed it on to my son and to those who have worked alongside me. As I observed earlier, it would have been so easy and acceptable for me to quit high school. The deck was stacked against me as it was against so many others. But I didn't quit! I was working for a man who had persisted beyond failure. Just being with him, riding alongside of him, made all the difference in how I thought and responded to the world around me.

When I left home for St. Louis, I was pumped for instant success; after all, I was no longer in the segregated south. My dreams were ambushed before I arrived. To settle for less would have been the easy way out. But I held on to my aspirations. Internal persistence became my constant companion when none of my new friends understood what was driving me. It would have been so easy to make wrong choices, lose my focus, and redefine my journey just to get along with others—and to ease the fear that shadowed my life. At times, it looked as if the lessons from the Ice House would be for naught. Fortunately for me, those lessons from the cab of uncle Cleve's truck were planted deeply and had taken root and would travel with me from St. Louis to the United States Air Force and back to the civilian world. In all my personal and professional endeavors from Stairmaster to banking, the decision to stick with my dream was there, but no place was it more evident than when looking back on my career to become a published author.

While in the Air Force, I found myself engaged in an endeavor that would take me beyond even my wildest aspirations.

In 1965, I started to write short stories about growing up on the Mississippi Delta. I kept them to myself until one of my friends, another Airman, Paul Demuniz, suggested that I try to get them published. He thought they were that good. So I started sending them out to every publisher and magazine imaginable and continued to do so after arriving in D.C. to begin my assignment at the 89th. There, I was privileged to be among the first Americans to actually work with computers—big machines that had their own rooms and where the technicians handling them wore white jackets as if they were surgeons. Being in the 89th also afforded me the opportunity to have a close-up look at Air Force One, the presidential plane. I actually boarded the plane, sat in the seat of power, and gingerly placed my hand on the "Red" phone that connected Russia and the United States.

*I found myself engaged in an
endeavor that would take me beyond
even my wildest aspirations.*

161

However, in spite of the excitement of my day job, my stories continued to be rejected. It seemed as if no one wanted to hear about a small town in the Mississippi Delta and about the ordinary people who lived there. I thought about quitting. I had enough rejection letters to support that notion.

My one friend, Paul, and some of the other guys who I was now taking classes with continued to encourage me to keep writing, while many of my other "goodtime" military buddies urged me to quit and to use my free time to have some fun for a change. It would have been so easy to follow their advice, but I had my small community of well-chosen buddies, who talked about the future, not about quitting. So, I continued to write. Something had shifted in my thinking a long time ago. The example of Uncle Cleve was close by and his resolve reminded me of what I needed to do. I needed to write. At the very least, the practice would make me a better writer.

It would in fact take years to achieve my goal of publication. There would be more rejection letters and a cross-country move back to Tulsa after I was discharged. I returned to school, and in my spare time, I continued to write. Even as the rejection slips continued, I was persistent.

Finally, twenty-four years after I wrote it, my first book, *Once Upon a Time When We Were Colored*, was published in 1989. The book is a first-person account of the cultural experience of southern blacks who lived behind the wall of legal segregation, providing many people their first look behind that way of life. I also became the first African American to receive the Mississippi Institute of Arts and Letters Award for nonfiction writing. My pride in this achievement, so hard won, was immense. I gave up a thousand times and continued a thousand more. But I had learned at an early age from an uncommon man not to quit. I had learned to keep cutting and selling that ice.

The book, which almost did not get published at all, became an official gift to President Mandela of South Africa.

Even with the book's publication, I was challenged. My publishers printed 3,000 copies and informed me that those copies would probably last for five years. I accepted that, knowing I had accomplished more than I could have imagined had I never left Glen Allan. Being an author had not been a specific aspiration, but once I started trying, I wanted to be successful. Suffice it to say that my publishers were wrong. It seemed the time was finally right for what I had to say. The book took off. Major newspapers across the nation—from the Chicago Tribune to the New York Times and the Boston Globe—embraced my small book about my Delta community. And the fans followed. Ordinary citizens thanked me for writing their story with grace and dignity. The book, which almost did not get published at all, became an official gift to President Mandela of South Africa.

I am glad I followed my heart and didn't give up. Soon these national reviews caught the attention of one of the producers for the "Phil Donahue Show." I was invited to be a guest—my first time visiting New York City! Even having completed a military career, I was nervous and apprehensive. My fears intensified while I waited in the studio's Green Room. The other guests were surrounded by their "people," and I had no one. I steeled myself for failure. It looked pretty imminent to me.

However, while on the stage before the live audience, Mr. Donahue picked up my book and began to read from it. Then he talked about it. And he kept going. He was wonderful. Needless to say, by the time I left New York that day I was known all over the Donahue television world. *Once Upon a Time When We Were Colored* went on to become a major motion picture and provided the foundational framework for our company today, a framework centered on the power of community as a workplace force multiplier—that extra energy that shows up to help you to achieve more than you planned as a result of being engaged in building and sustaining community.

I have since written nine other books including, *The Last Train North*, a Pulitzer Prize nominee. To contemplate quitting is human. To persist and not give up is entrepreneurial. I learned so much from Uncle Cleve, and his wisdom continues to feed my thinking. Because of his involvement in my life, I learned to ignore rejection letters and to keep writing and believing in myself. While working at the Ice House, I learned that no rewards are handed out for quitting. I saw Uncle Cleve persevere. I realized that I could do no less. I learned not to fold. This is the mindset I embrace today.

THE TIMELESS APPLICATION

Entrepreneurship is a mindset. It is a mindset that can empower ordinary people to create extraordinary lives. It is a mindset that exposes opportunity and ignites ambition. It is a mindset that fosters innovation and initiative, curiosity and lifelong learning, as well as the self-reliance and resourcefulness of which we are all capable.

And, as Uncle Cleve showed, there is no magic bullet that will enable you to succeed. Entrepreneurship is not for those who seek to "get rich quick." There is no proven step-by-step formula that will guarantee our success. But there is the right mindset to get you on track.

An entrepreneurial mindset does not require unique abilities or a rare talent. It does not require lots of money or an Ivy League MBA. It does not require anything you don't already have. It does, however, require hard work, perseverance, and determination.

Our ability to persevere is perhaps the most powerful ability we possess. It may also be the most undervalued. And it is an ability that many of us do not recognize or value. It is one we often overlook.

Success is a dream for millions throughout the world, and almost all of us are willing to work hard to reach for a better life. Yet our efforts can only take us as far as our understanding, and we often mistakenly assign success to things that are beyond our control.

We also often fall prey to popular myths and misconceptions about entrepreneurs and what it really takes to succeed. We imagine that those who have succeeded had some advantage that is, for whatever reason not available to us, and we completely overlook the hard work, the months and years of uncertainty and setbacks, the perseverance and determination that often creates the core of an entrepreneur's success.

Without realizing it, by adopting these beliefs, we may be letting ourselves off the hook. We may also be blinding ourselves to opportunities as well as our own untapped potential.

Some simply give up too easily. Rather than finding another solution or a better approach, they just give up. They perceive obstacles as dead ends rather than problems that must be solved. Without realizing it, they accept limitations that they actually may be able to overcome.

Sadly, many never try.

165

Others expect it to be easy. They convince themselves that the only thing they need to be successful is a good idea and then their worries will be over and everything will take care of itself.

Yet, as any entrepreneur will tell you, there is no secret to success. There is no proven formula or money-back guarantee. Being an entrepreneur is hard work, by most accounts, 1% inspiration coupled with 99% perspiration. And, when it comes right down to it, perseverance and determination often hold the key

Daunting as this may seem, entrepreneurs choose a different approach to their work, one that ignites their ambition and fosters their innate abilities that, when added to a work ethic, enables them to succeed.

Rather than something to be avoided, entrepreneurs approach their work with passion, enthusiasm, and a desire to make a difference in the world. Faced with daily challenges, their minds are ready to cope with whatever barriers they may encounter.

Inner-directed and future-focused, they do not wait to be told what to do. Rather than trading time for money, entrepreneurs are constantly searching for new ideas that will enable them to expand their world.

Free of policies and procedures that thwart innovation and initiative, entrepreneurs see problems as opportunities and are always in search of solutions. Unencumbered by narrowly defined job descriptions, they surround themselves with others who are inner-directed, goal oriented, and willing to work hard.

Rather than buy into get-rich-quick schemes, they are solution-oriented and understand that success will come about by solving problems. They comprehend the power of knowledge combined with effort. They rarely blame others, choosing instead to learn from their mistakes.

166

Yet among the habits that enable them to succeed, perhaps none is more powerful than their willingness to persevere. Entrepreneurs simply refuse to fold.

The ability to persevere, like the other mindset lessons Uncle Cleve left behind, does not require special talent or unique abilities. It is a habit that comes about with the shift in our awareness—a shift that must be followed by a change in our behavior.

Expecting success to be easy is a mistake. In fact, success as an entrepreneur may be the hardest thing you will ever do. Through sheer perseverance and determination, it may also be the most rewarding.

Clifton Taulbert and Gary Schoeniger

WHO OWNS THE ICE HOUSE? *Eight Life Lessons From An Unlikely Entrepreneur*

LOOKING BEYOND THE ICE HOUSE TO YOUR FUTURE

*"The wave of the future is not the conquest of the world by a
single dogmatic creed, but the liberation of the diverse energies
of free nations and free men."*
—JOHN F. KENNEDY

FROM CLIFTON

Thank you for reading *Who Owns the Ice House?* I was honored to take you to my hometown and to the place I worked as a young boy. At the time of my employment, I had no idea that I was living and working in the presence of a man whose life lessons could be of value to people around the world. Uncle Cleve was just an ordinary man who had tapped into an extraordinary way of living his life. It was evident to all of those around him. I knew he was different. I admired him. Even after leaving home, upon my periodic returns, I continued to seek his nod of approval for many of my life's efforts.

However, it was Gary who envisioned this project, challenging me to look beyond my personal life with Uncle Cleve and to see him as not just my mentor/employer from years ago, but as a uniquely successful entrepreneur with wisdom applicable to our day and time. I knew that Gary knew entrepreneurs. Finding and sharing their stories has been his life's work and, as you know, searching for entrepreneurial stories occasioned our first meeting. When Gary heard about Uncle Cleve and the Ice House, he insisted that I bring his story to that conference in Austin.

As reluctant as I was about revealing the roots of my success, it turned out that Uncle Cleve was right at home in Austin. As I told his story from the perspective of an unlikely entrepreneur, I also felt as if I was turning on lights within my own head. I began to see him in an entirely different light, much in the way Gary did when he had first heard Uncle Cleve's story. What I experienced at the Ice House and what Gary gleaned from my story became the impetus for the creation of this project. Sometimes, it takes a nudge from another person and looking through the rearview mirror to truly assess our life's journey and to see the possibilities in it that exist for others. What you have just finished reading is all about possibilities that exist—oftentimes right within our reach.

When I left home in 1963, Uncle Cleve was still serving our community. Sadly, however, while I was away serving in the 89th Presidential Wing of the United States Air Force, I received the phone call that Uncle Cleve, who had been ill, had passed away. I was unable to get home to his funeral, but all of his sons and their families were there including his youngest son, my cousin Joe. We had grown up together. Although he is no longer with us, the impact of his presence continues to be remembered. His wisdom will not be forgotten and when our families gather, there will always be stories about the Iceman who always drove under the speed limit. And with this book, we have extended his reach further.

As you move your life forward—aspiring entrepreneur, restless student, or someone who is looking to transform the way you are living life—this is my heartfelt wish for you. I want this project to ignite a spark within you, one that refuses to be placed under a bushel or snuffed out, but one that burns brightly. I want you to be everything of which you are capable. Start your own business if that's your desire. Will it be easy? Of course not, but your efforts will not go unrewarded. Finish your education. Discover your potential to achieve beyond what others might think of you. Turn your life around if that's what needs to happen—and leave the negative past behind. Life transformation is possible, and you don't have to be thirteen when it starts. You can begin at any age.

As you can see from my experiences, your life can provide value for yourself and for others on so many different levels. Embrace these eight lessons from the Ice House about the entrepreneurial mindset and the significance they can have for your life today no matter where you find yourself.

In this book, we took you back in time with real stories from my small hometown—stories meant to engage your thinking and to reveal what is possible in spite of challenging odds. We didn't stop at the Ice House. Drawing from over two decades of entrepreneurial experience, Gary carefully and thoughtfully pulled out the key points from each of my stories. Furthermore, he made sure that you understood as we do, that what I learned while riding in the cab of my uncle's truck is applicable to your life today. I trust that you have highlighted specific notes throughout this book—capturing those special points that spoke to you, those points that

Clifton Taulbert and Gary Schoeniger

made you stop and say: "Wow, I get it!" In Gary's sections of each chapter, he takes you beyond the heat and humidity of the Delta into the world where you live and where your aspirations can initiate a new life. I see this book as an extension of Uncle Cleve's cab—no longer crowded with oily rags and old newspapers, but with plenty of room for you to hear his voice and to embrace his everlasting wisdom.

What I experienced was timeless and universal. I know this now. I didn't at the time. I was too young then. Uncle Cleve's personal commitment to success, lived out in front of me, shifted my perspective of how I could live my life. He never once said, "Clifton, watch me, I am shifting your thinking." He just lived differently and consistently in my presence. The change in my thinking constituted a subtle but important shift. It took place while we were both doing hard work, lifting and cutting big blocks of ice and serving our customers. But it was a powerful shift. It was powerful enough to make me realize that I could be different when at the time everything was driven by tradition and low expectations. Generations before I was born, society had already decided the course of my life—where I would live and the type of work I would do and in so doing sought to hijack my imagination. When Uncle Cleve hired me, he showed me a different way of making a living and, over time, a different way of living my life. I didn't have to catch Mr. Walter's field truck.

In this book, the field truck became a metaphor for being stuck in the same rut—doing what others expect, becoming satisfied, afraid to move out beyond what we have become accustomed to. Uncle Cleve wanted more for me. Over time, I wanted more for myself. I realized that the future included me.

Now I want more for you. I want you to unleash your potential, to fly as high as your wings will take you. Don't settle! Just as Uncle Cleve prepared me for life beyond the Ice

House, his timeless and universal lessons will do the same for you. I believe this with all my heart. I encourage you to see the world as yours.

This is not empty rhetoric or overstated exuberance. I do not pretend to have the "hidden secret" to success. Gary and I have both walked this path ourselves as entrepreneurs. We have had exciting days and days of heartbreak, but our journey continues. And we have met countless others who have embraced the entrepreneurial mindset—ordinary people who have accomplished extraordinary things by following these basic Ice House lessons, by tapping into their potential and solving problems for themselves and for others. The benefits of doing so have resulted in phenomenal success for them as it has for the both of us. We want no less for you. The world needs you. There is an endless array of problems waiting to be solved, questions needing your answers. Your passion is needed. Your talents and your abilities are needed. This is your time.

And there's even more available to help you as this project goes far beyond the book you've just read. This project is a 21st century endeavor. Gary has harnessed technology to take the project to the next level with the online course—easily accessible and affordable. I can't wait for you to hear his voice on just how this multimedia online course will change your life. I invite you to embrace the power of the entrepreneurial mindset and transform your life as you become immersed in the companion learning initiative of *Who Owns the Ice House?* online.

And it is Gary, with his steadfast entrepreneurial mindset, that you have to thank for initiating and participating in this incredible idea.

Clifton Taulbert and Gary Schoeniger

FROM GARY

"Long before the word 'entrepreneur' became popular,
the concept still existed."

These were among the first words Clifton Taulbert uttered
during our chance interview as he began to describe the entrepreneurial influence and the life-lessons he gained as a young
boy growing up in the Mississippi Delta during the height of
legal segregation.

Needless to say, I was immediately captivated by the
power of Clifton's story and the impact Uncle Cleve had made
on his life.

As an entrepreneur, I have long been fascinated with
entrepreneurship—specifically the mindset of successful
entrepreneurs: the underlying beliefs and the behaviors that
enable them to succeed. How did they recognize opportunities
that the rest of us overlooked? And what is it that led them
to accomplish so much with so little? Were they born with a
unique ability or is an entrepreneurial mindset something we
can all learn to apply?

Clifton's story of Uncle Cleve immediately reminded
me of Jason, a young boy who crossed my path more than a
decade earlier.

Jason was just eleven when I met him. He was a foster
child who had been living with a friend. I was a single dad and
entrepreneur with my own responsibilities, yet I could foresee
the downward trajectory of Jason's life, and I wanted more for
him. I wanted him to see a brighter future. I wanted him to see
the power of possibilities and the potential that an entrepreneurial mindset could provide.

And, just as Uncle Cleve made a place for young Clifton,
I made a place for Jason.

After folding him into our household, I began to look for ways to change his perspective. I saw that he was settling for less and that his outlook needed to be changed. I introduced him to an opportunity to start his own small business. I figured it would spark his initiative and show him that success was possible, something mere words and telling cannot always accomplish.

With nothing more than a bucket and a broom, an old Shop-Vac and a few printed flyers, Jason set out offering to clean construction sites for local home builders. Although he was uncertain and somewhat afraid, he set out, and through persistence, he found his first customer. Soon, by doing what he said he would do, Jason found success and his business began to grow. It was an entrepreneurial experience that had a profound impact on his life.

After graduating from high school with a Presidential Citation for Academic Achievement, and after serving in the United State Marine Corps, Jason is now enrolled in college and traveling the world, well on his way to making a meaningful contribution to all of our lives.

Although he does not yet own another business, the entrepreneurial mindset changed his perspective and gave him a glimpse of his own untapped potential.

As of the printing of this book, I have interviewed hundreds of successful entrepreneurs across America—from mom-and-pop startups to Inc. 500 winners. Some were highly educated, others barely finished high school. Some were experts in their field. Others had little or no experience at all. For some, becoming an entrepreneur was a lifelong dream. For others it was a matter of survival.

Most started with little or nothing. They all overcame setbacks, adversity, and failures that ultimately enabled them to succeed. Each of their stories contained valuable knowledge and insights as a mindset began to emerge.

I now realize the same lessons that empowered Uncle Cleve and Jason are the same lessons that have empowered some of the most successful entrepreneurs of our time. I now understand that entrepreneurship is a mindset that can empower ordinary people to do extraordinary things.

Clifton's story captures the essence of an entrepreneurial mindset and the unlimited opportunities it can provide. They are lessons that do not require money, special training, or unique abilities. They are indeed timeless and universal truths that anyone can apply.

Regardless of where you are right now, the entrepreneurial mindset can empower you to create the life you have imagined. It is a mindset that will enable you to recognize opportunities that are within your reach. It is a mindset that can empower you to triumph over adversity and to make a greater contribution during your lifetime.

The great advances in life rarely come about as the result of doing more of what we are already doing. They come about as the result of a shift in our awareness followed by a change in our behavior.

It is my sincere hope that this story will inspire you to take action; that it will shift your awareness and ignite something within you that will compel you to succeed—wherever you are in your life and in whatever you choose to do.

ACKNOWLEDGEMENTS

CLIFTON TAULBERT

When you finally finish writing a book, you realize that more than one person was involved in the process. A good book is truly a collaborative effort. First and foremost, I want to thank my writing partner, Gary for insisting that I bring the "Ice House and Uncle Cleve" to life for this generation. Gary kept wanting more of the story. Hopefully each person who reads this book will be moved by the depth of the stories I sought to bring into their lives and become motivated to make these timeless lessons their very own.

It goes without saying that much thanks go to my wife, Barbara who gave up her time with me so that I could write and rewrite. I'd like to thank Doug Decker, a member of our team who probably knows the book by memory. He had to read it so many times. And lastly, I want to thank Thom Ruhe and the Kauffman Foundation for embracing the possibility that a universal entrepreneurial story lived at an Ice House in Glen Allan, Mississippi.

Clifton Taulbert and Gary Schoeniger

GARY SCHOENIGER

This book represents a significant milestone on a long journey and I owe a tremendous debt of gratitude to those who unselfishly gave of themselves to encourage and support our efforts and make this book possible.

First, I would like to thank my partner Mike Sutyak, who believed in my ideas, took a chance and put his life on hold to help make this happen. I will be forever grateful to Clifton Taulbert for his intentional unselfishness and his willingness to share his personal story with two strangers from Cleveland, Ohio. I too would like to thank Thom Ruhe, of the Kauffman Foundation, who not only believed in us, but pushed us to help make this project the best that it could be. I would like to thank my friends Mike Baird, Bill Fellows, Kip Marlow and so many others who believed in our ideas and helped us keep the dream alive.

To my sons Samuel and Owen, I will always be grateful for their tolerance of my entrepreneurial endeavors. And lastly to Karen, without whose kindness, strength and support, this book would never have been possible.